CW01654853

First published 2009.

Cover design, photography and illustrations by Gary Fabbri, Malin Fabbri and Peter Wiklund.

Published by
AlternativePhotography.com
Vikingagatan 10
113 42 Stockholm
Sweden.

ISBN: 978-91-633-4380-3

For further information go to:
http://www.AlternativePhotography.com/PinholeToPrint.html

alternative photography

USE THIS BOOKLET to guide you from drilling your first pinhole to printing your first pinhole photograph.

The authors

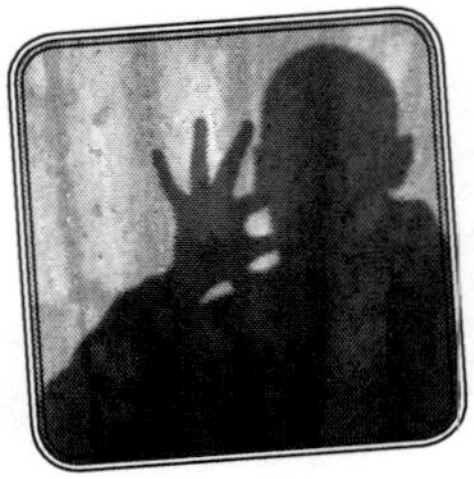

GARY FABBRI grew up in Rhode Island, USA. He moved to London after college to work as a writer/director. He has created award winning short films, television adverts and programs. Experimentation with visual media, pinhole and alternative processes lead to writing *Blueprint to cyanotypes* and *From pinhole to print.* Gary is now a Creative Director and runs his own company, Shed9, in Stockholm. See www.Shed9.com

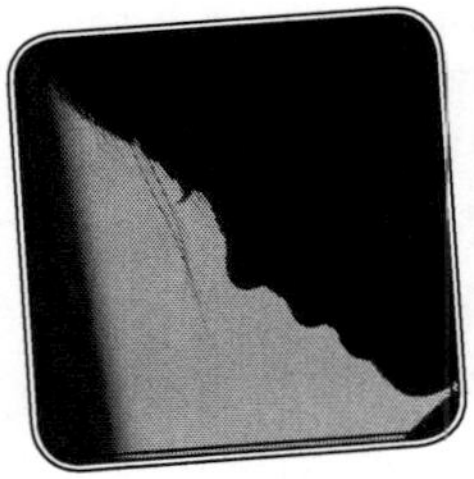

MALIN FABBRI moved from Sweden to London to study. She earned an MA in Design at Central St. Martin's and is an authority in alternative photographic processes. She has worked professionally with big media names like Time magazine and CNBC Europe. In 1999 she started - and is still the editor of AlternativePhotography.com. She is the co-author of *Blueprint to cyanotypes*, *From pinhole to print*, and the editor of *Alternative Photography: Art and Artists, Edition I*, a collection of artists working with historic processes today. See www.AlternativePhotography.com

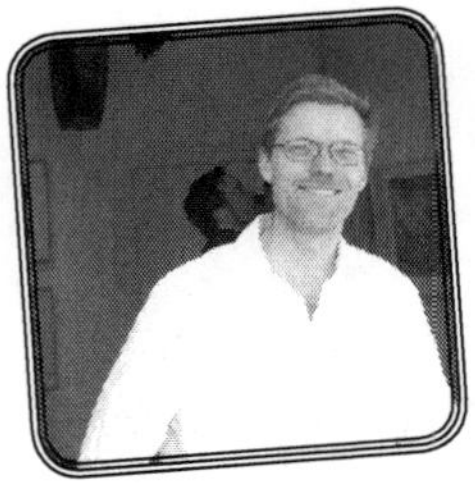

PETER WIKLUND started taking pinhole photographs in the early 1990s, after discovering the technique in *The Pinhole Journal* (R.I.P.). He uses a variety of cameras and materials; film, paper and Polaroids. He has exhibited his photographs frequently in galleries all over the world. Peter lives and works in Stockholm, Sweden, writing, making photographs and holding pinhole workshops. See www.PeterPinhole.com.

Why pinhole?

One of the best things about pinhole photography is its simplicity. Almost any container that can be made 'light-tight' can be turned into a pinhole camera.

Building your own camera is not only a great way to learn the true basics of photography, it is also incredibly fun to create something from scratch, that can take a photo. The world may be going digital, and it is fun and spontaneous to take a picture with your phone, but there is a mystery in taking a photograph with a pinhole camera, and a thrill in developing your own print in the darkroom.

Depth of field

Pinhole photographs have many interesting qualities, including a virtually infinite depth of field. This means that everything in the image, no matter how close or distant, lies in the same focal plane.

If you place an apple in the foreground and a tree stands far away in the background, then both the apple and the tree will be in focus. With an ordinary camera, either the apple or the tree would be in focus, not both. This 'infinite look' is quite unique to pinhole cameras, and can help you create very startling images.

Long exposure times

It may be possible to adjust your ordinary camera to have long or short exposure times, but long exposure times are part and parcel of pinholing.

Exposure times can range from several seconds to several minutes. Taking advantage of this time allows you to produce a multitude of blur effects as the subjects of your photographs move, or as you move the camera.

Timeless quality

Pinholes have a 'timeless' quality, that makes you want to release your creative potential. It is sometimes hard to tell whether the image was taken yesterday or a hundred years ago. Imperfections such as reflections and light leaks become values in a pinhole image. Pinhole cameras simply see the world differently from the way our eyes see it.

Limitations lead to freedom

At first glance the pinhole camera may seem too simple to offer versatility to an experienced photographer. But, as is often the case, limitations release creativity.

Pinhole history - a few key moments in the

The first known permanent photograph, *View from window at Le Gras*, was taken by Joseph Nicephore Niépce in 1826. It represented a huge advancement in the development of photosensitive material. But the type of camera he used to create the image had existed for centuries.

The camera obscura, Latin for *dark room*, took a natural optical phenomenon and put it in a box. Many tales have been told about cave dwellers, hundreds of thousands of years ago, observing pinhole images on the back walls of their caves. These projections were most likely created when a tiny hole allowed just enough light through to cast a picture of the outside world onto the dark stone.

The camera obscura made it possible for ancient Chinese and Greeks to observe the sun. It was instrumental for artists during the Italian Renaissance who struggled to create realistic linear perspective. And it was the only type of camera available for Niépce to take that first photo. In fact, it was most likely the reason he tried to capture that elusive image from his window at Le Gras in the first place.

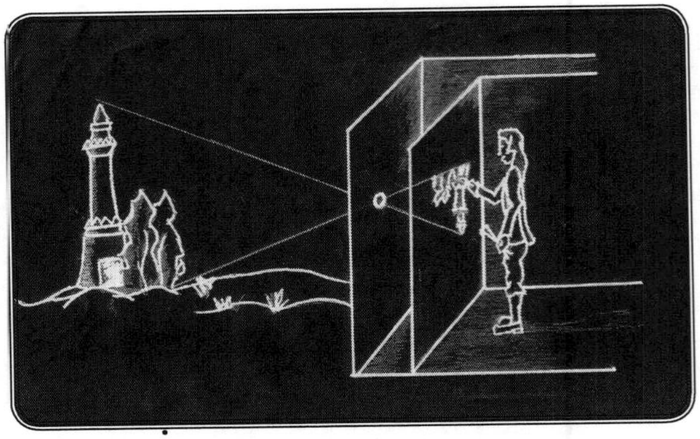

An artist using an early camera obscura.

1544

Dutch mathematician and physician Gemma Frisius illustrated an eclipse using a camera obscura.

16th century

Leonardo da Vinci describes a camera obscura: "you make a small round hole and an illuminated object will project an image through that hole and be visible inside the dwelling on the opposite wall".

1619

Christopher Scheiner made a camera obscura with a lens to correct the inverted image.

1725

Johann Schultze, a German physicist discovered that silver salts reacted to light.

discovery of camera obscura & photosensitivity

1834

Englishman William Henry Fox Talbot, produced paper coated with silver chloride and exposed it in a camera obscura.

1839

Sir John Herschel discovers that hypo can fix images. He coins the words 'photography', 'positive', 'negative' and 'snap shot'.

1839

Daguerre publicly announces the invention of daguerreotypes in France.

1850

Despite the new lenses, some people still continued using pinhole cameras. Sir David Brewster, an English scientist, is thought to be the first to use the word 'pinhole'.

1829

Louis Jacques Mandé Daguerre, invented the Diorama - a panoramic light show used for entertainment. He wanted to find a way for images to "record themselves". He sought out Niépce and together they abandoned Heliography and began to research silver iodide.

1802

Thomas Wedgewood experimented with silver chloride on leather and paper. He produced photographs by contact printing images of leaves, exposing them to sunlight.

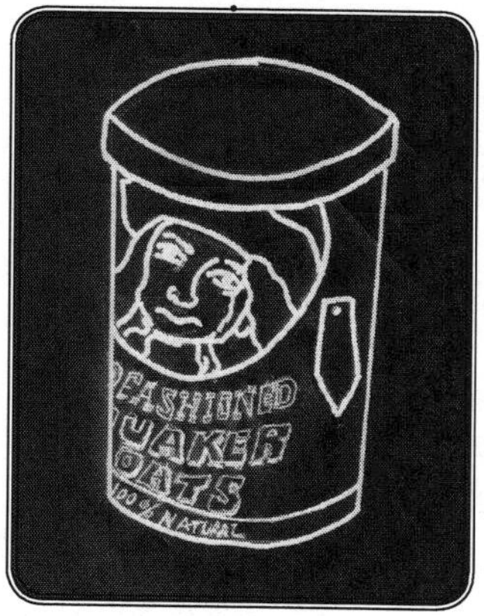

Today people make pinhole cameras from all types of containers.

How a pinhole camera works

One thing that inspires many pinhole photographers is the craft of building their own cameras. Finding new materials or a perfect box can be like uncovering a hidden treasure.

The pinhole camera is amazing in its simplicity. It is, in its most basic form, a light proof container with light sensitive material at one end and a pinhole at the other.

Pinhole cameras rely on the fact that light travels in straight lines – a principle called the *rectilinear theory of light*. This makes the image appear upside down in the camera.

If the dimensions of your camera and the size of your pinhole are correct you can take a photograph that will compete on a technical level with a photograph from your digital SLR camera.

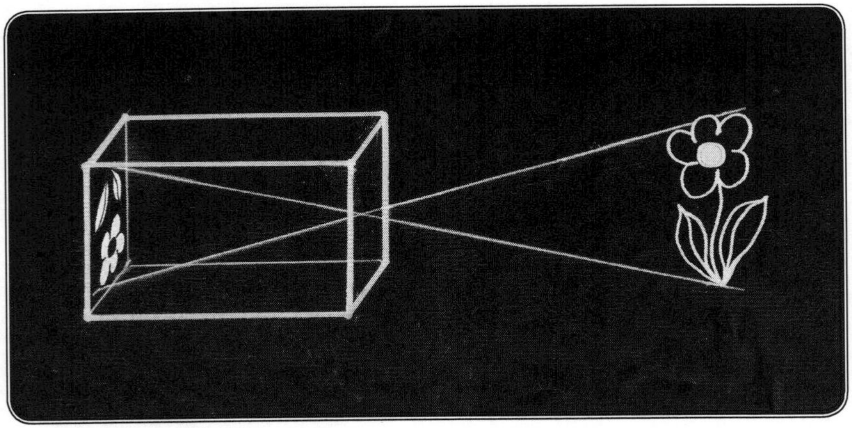

A small pinhole generally produces sharper images than a larger one. However, if the pinhole is too small, light waves may be scattered slightly at the edges of the pinhole and cause distortion or loss of focus.

Smaller holes also increase exposure times, since they will let less light into the camera.

Pinhole cameras are characterized by the fact that they do not have a lens. If a camera has a lens, it is NOT a pinhole camera.

When the shutter is opened, light shines through to imprint an image on photographic paper or film placed at the back of the camera.

Focal length

The focal length of your pinhole camera is the distance between the pinhole at the front of the camera and the paper or film at the back of the camera.

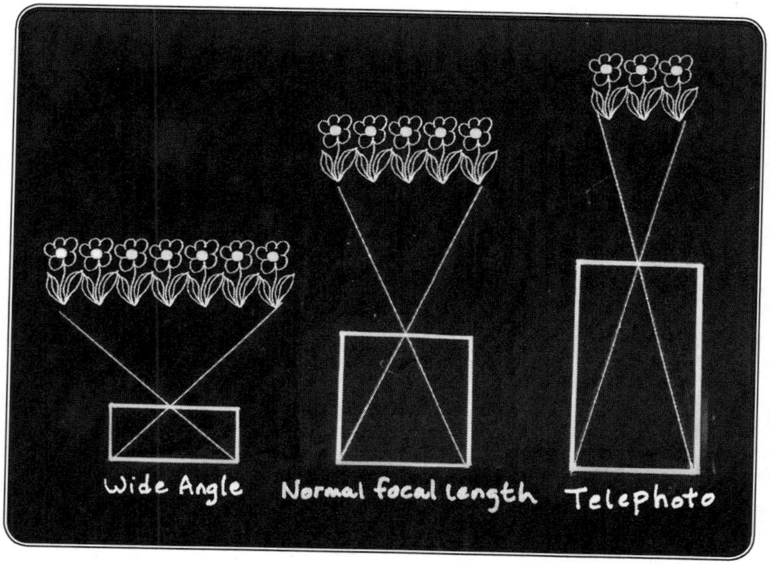

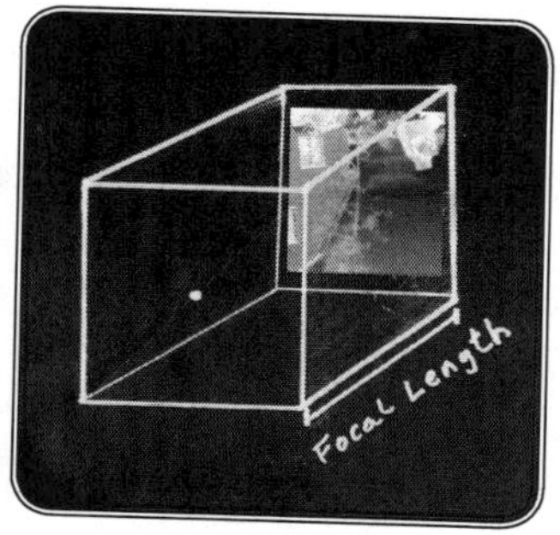

Left: A focal length about equal length to the diagonal size of the paper or film is a normal focal length. A shorter focal length is called a wide-angle, and a significantly longer is referred to as telephoto.

Below: The three photographs show the different effects when varying the focal lengths. The image on the left was taken with a pinhole camera with a focal length of 15 mm, the one in the middle used 30 mm and the one on the right 60 mm, all taken on 120-film / 2 1/4" film.

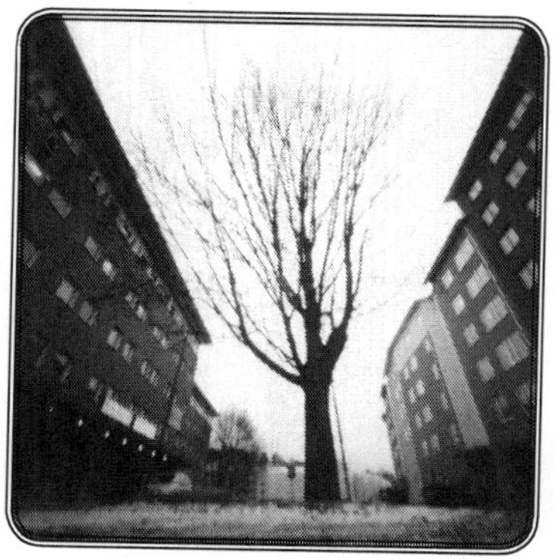

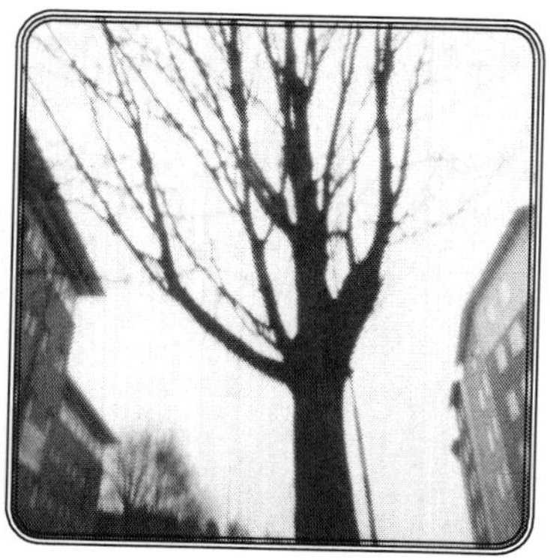

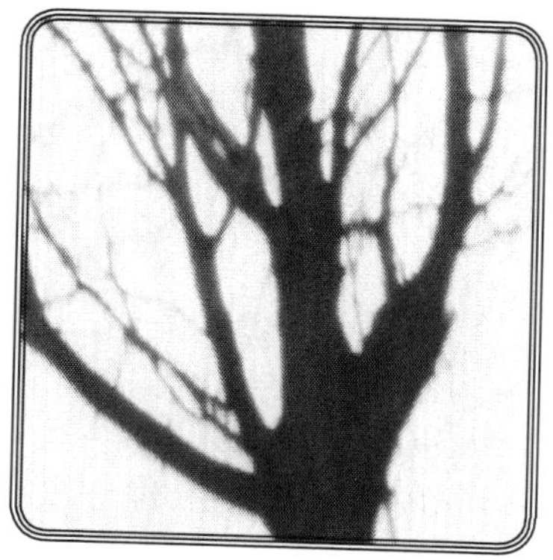

Vignettes

When the light enters the pinhole at the front of the camera, it is projected onto the paper or film at the back in a circle. The diameter of the image circle is roughly three and a half times the focal length. You may end up with a black vignette around the image if you have a shorter focal length. And this may be exactly what you want.

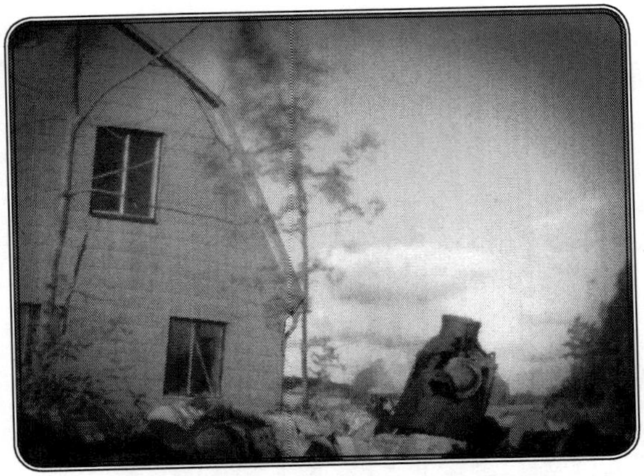

Focal length facts

Short focal length

- Wide angle
- Short exposure times

Long focal length

- Telephoto
- Long exposure times

The vignette appears because light is forced to travel further to the outer edges of the circle leaving it underexposed. If you don't want this effect, make sure the camera doesn't require paper that is larger than approximately twice its focal length.

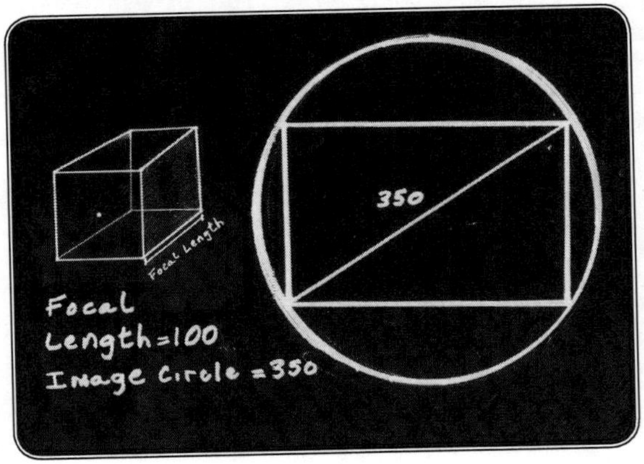

A camera with a 100 mm focal length will produce an image circle with a diameter of 350 mm. A small image circle causes light fall off and vignetting at the edges of an image.

The intensity of the light in your camera decreases as you extend the length of the camera. The light will be stronger nearest the hole and gradually weaken as it continues towards the back of the camera. This means that you will need longer exposure times for telephoto cameras.

A camera with a focal length of 3 inches will produce an image with a diameter of approximately 10.5 inches.

Make a pinhole camera – from a can

A PINHOLE CAMERA can be made out of almost anything that you can make light tight. Cans, cookie jars and boxes have perfect pinhole potential. But other, more unusual items like a walnut, a red pepper and even someone's mouth have been transformed into pinhole cameras.

The most important feature is that it is possible to make the camera light tight. If you want to use a box, pick a sturdy one with a tight top. If you use a can, try finding one with an opaque lid, or take steps to make the lid light proof. Using a square container will give you a flat film plane, a curved one will result in a bent film plane. Creating your own camera will be a lot more fun if you start with a good container.

Let's make a simple pinhole camera starting with a can. Search your cupboards, you will most likely have one at home already.

Materials list

Need to have - without these it will be hard to make a camera:

- Can or box
- Scissors and a hobby knife
- Ruler
- Flat black paint & brushes, paint in a spray can, or black paper
- Black tape (preferably photographic tape, lots of it!)
- Glue
- Thin metal, like an aluminium can
- Fine sandpaper or abrasive cloth
- Thin needles
- Cork or eraser to hold needle
- Photo paper, RC paper

Nice to have - extra bits that will make life easier:

- Scanner, projector or micrometer for measuring needles and holes
- Backing paper from 120-film, great for covering light leaks
- Light meter, for determining the right exposure time
- Darkroom bag, or light proof bags for changing paper outside the darkroom

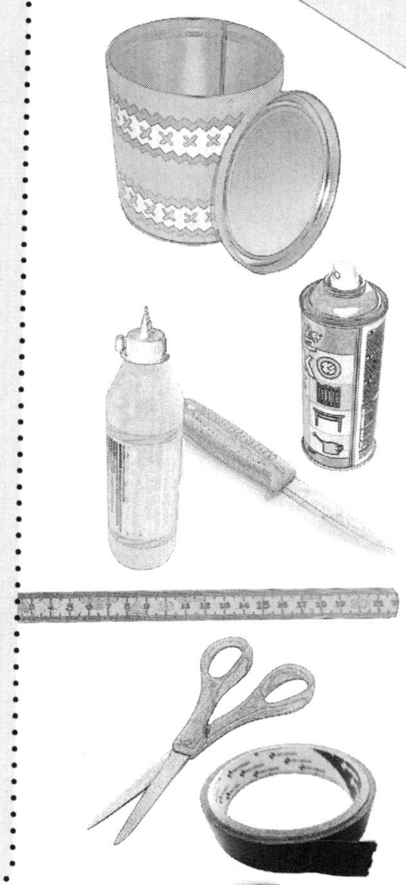

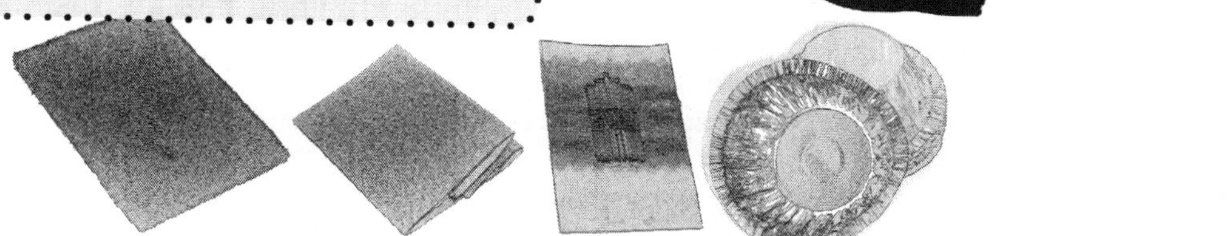

Building the camera in six simple steps

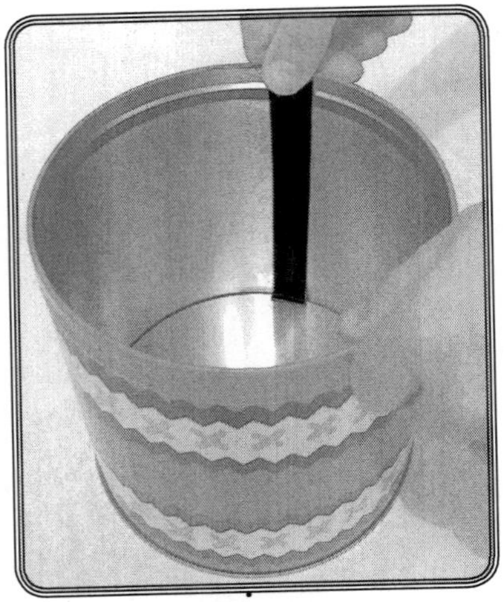

Step 1. Light proofing

Your can is probably not light proof. Hold it up to the light and you will see any obvious light leaks. A metal can will probably have fewer light leaks than a cardboard box. Leaks are a standard dilemma for pinholers, but nothing that black tape can't fix.

Tape all folds and corners on the outside of the container.

Tape all inside corners and joints if you suspect they are leaking light. Hold the container up to the light, to make sure you can't see any obvious light leaks. Do the same with the lid. If using a cardboard box, try finding one where the lid comes down a fair amount and fits tightly. If it does not fit, find a better box, or try making a U-shaped lip for the lid.

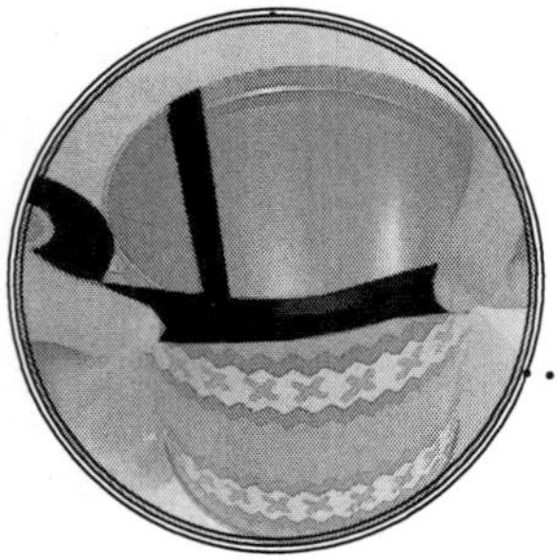

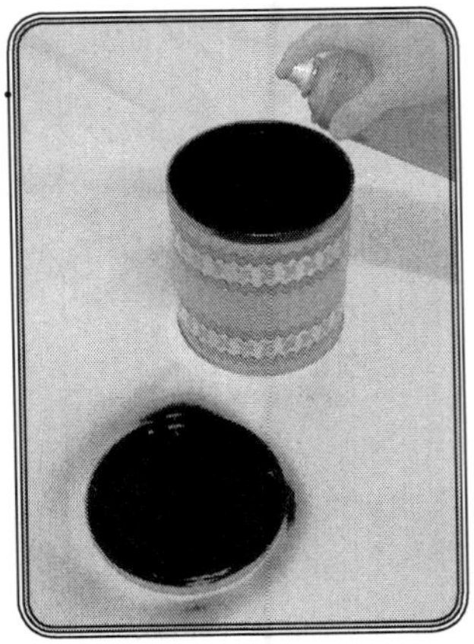

Cover your work surface. Spray both the inside of the lid and the can with flat black paint. Do not use gloss paint. A shiny layer of paint will reflect light inside your camera, affecting your final image. Leave the paint to dry and spray it again. If you are using a Pringles or an oatmeal can with a transparent plastic lid, it also has to be blackened properly. Alternatively, you can glue mat black paper to the inside of the can and lid. Both the paint and the paper should be as non-reflective as possible.

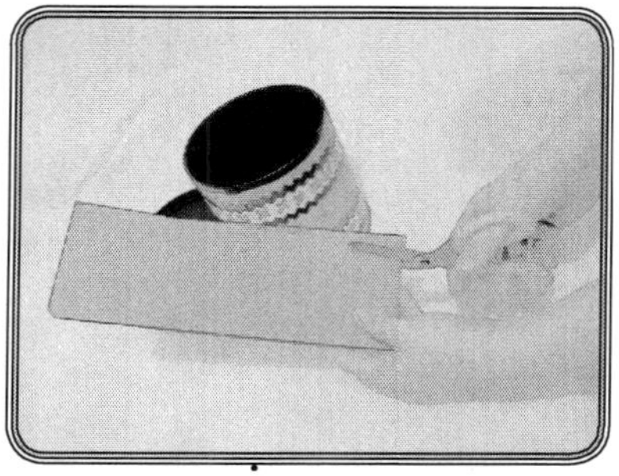

STEP 2: MAKING A PAPER HOLDER

While you are waiting for the paint to dry, make a paper holder that will hold the photo paper at the back of the camera.
Take a piece of thick cardboard and cut four strips. The strips should be slightly shorter than the height of the can, so they don't hold the lid open.

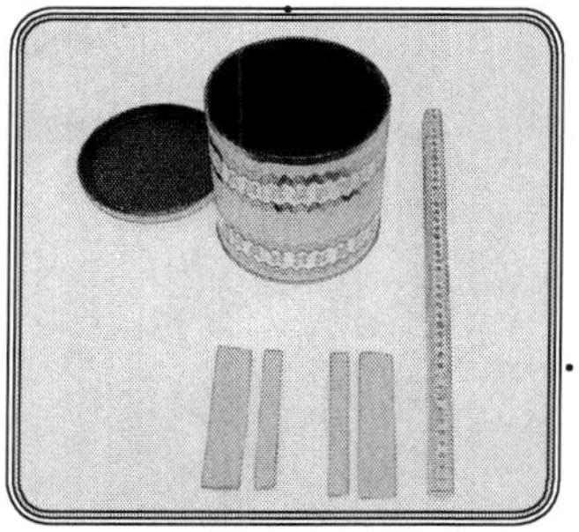

Cut two strips that are roughly 1 cm / 0.5 inches wide, and two that are 2 cm / 1 inch wide.

Glue the thinner pieces on top of the thicker ones.

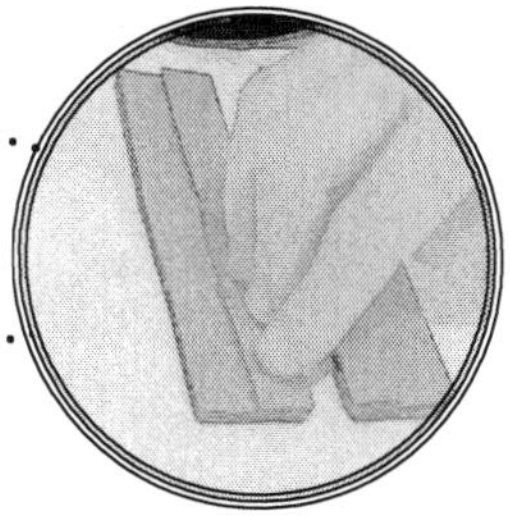

Take a piece of paper that is the same size as your photo paper. Turn the can over, so that the paper lies flat when you load it. Glue the cardboard pieces in place just outside the outer edges of the paper.

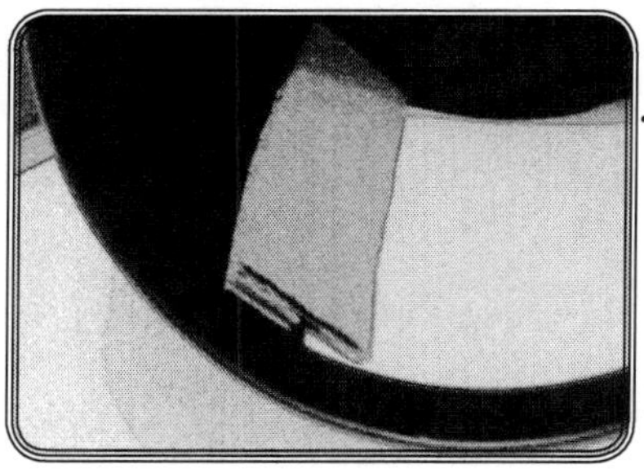

A slot is made for the paper to fit into. Once the glue has dried you can slide a piece of paper into the holder to test it.

If you are using a metal can to make your pinhole camera, you can use two fridge magnets to hold your photo paper in place.

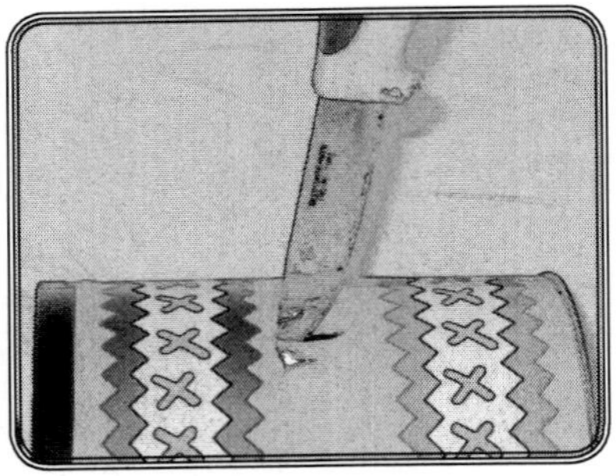

Step 3. Making the hole for the pinhole

To make the hole in the front of the can, you need to find the center of the can. Measure carefully. The hole also needs to be exactly opposite the paper holder you just made.

Use a utility knife to cut the hole in the can - it shouldn't do too much damage to the knife. If it is a heavy duty metal can, a drill can be used, though make sure the hole is not too small. A pair of scissors can be used if the container is made of cardboard. Once you have made the hole, you are ready to make a pinhole.

Step 4. Making the pinhole

Use a thin metal sheet for the pinhole, a baking tray, aluminium drink can or similar material will work. Many pinholers use a thin brass sheet called a 'shim'. Cut a small square or circle. You can use ordinary household scissors for this, although it will make them blunt quite quickly.

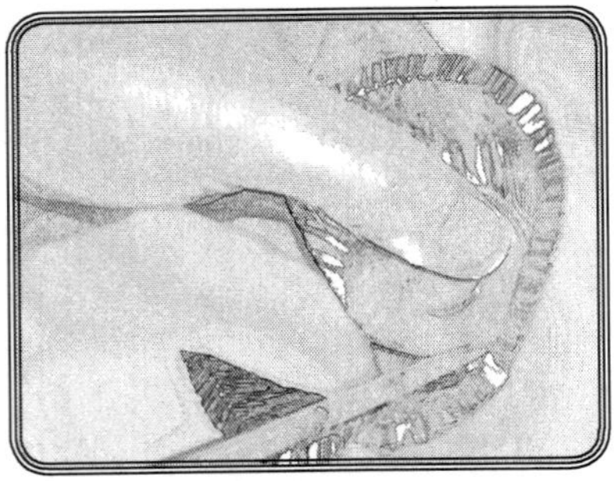

Pinhole material

Some items you can use for the pinhole:

- Brass or aluminium shim
- Disposable aluminium baking pan
- Any metal sheet of tin, brass or silver
- Soft drink can

Cooking foil can be used, but is very thin and rips easily.

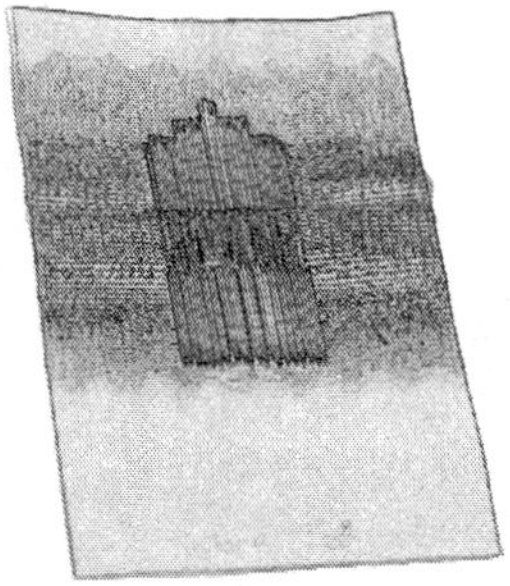

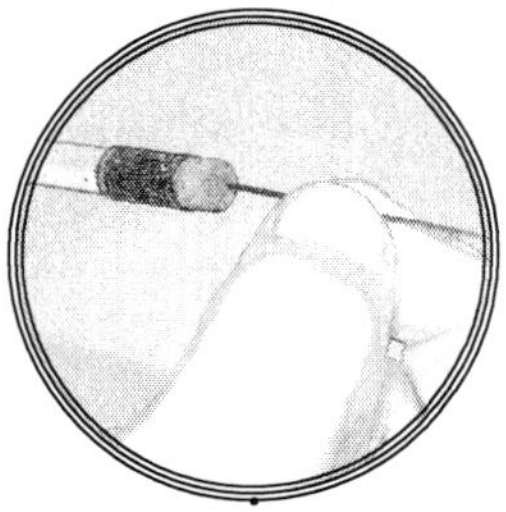

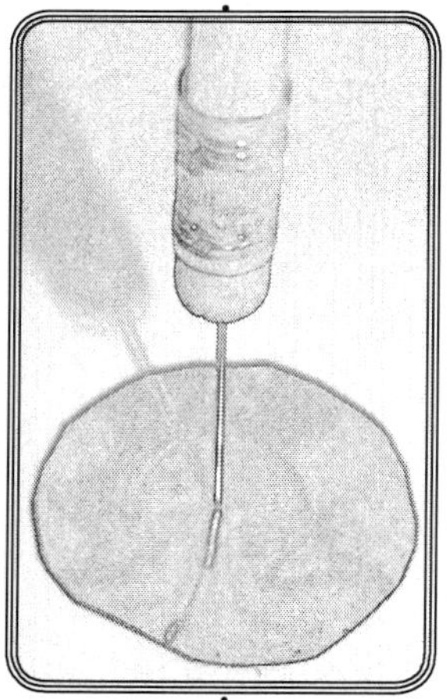

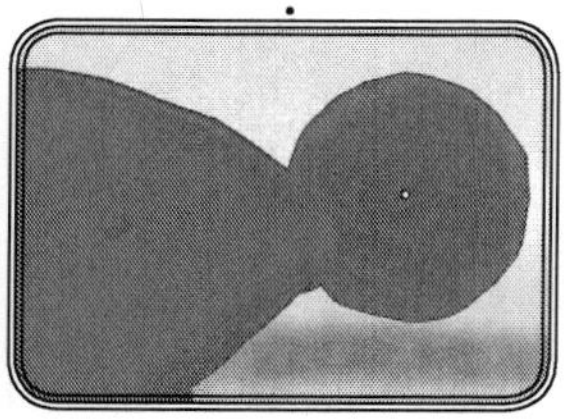

Chose the needle that will make the pinhole. If you can find needles that are numbered in the traditional way, you can determine the size of the hole using the guide to the right. Or, measure them with a micrometer. Most people don't have micrometers these days, but they still work, and can be found on eBay.

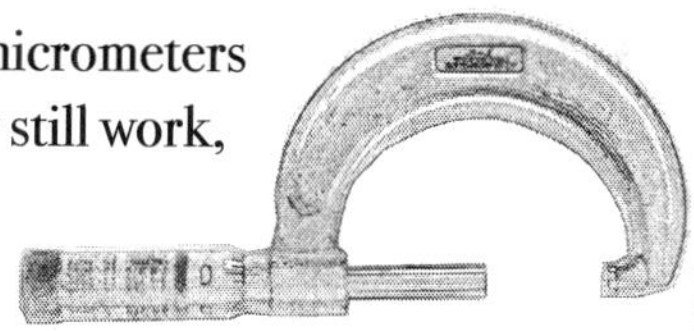

Needle size guide

Needle number	Diameter in inches	Diameter in millimeter
1	0.046″	1.17 mm
2	0.043″	1.09 mm
3	0.040″	1.02 mm
4	0.037″	0.94 mm
5	0.034″	0.86 mm
6	0.030″	0.76 mm
7	0.027″	0.69 mm
8	0.024″	0.61 mm
9	0.021″	0.53 mm
10	0.018″	0.46 mm
11	0.016″	0.42 mm
12	0.014″	0.35 mm
13	0.012″	0.30 mm
14	0.011″	0.28 mm
15	0.010″	0.25 mm

You may also use acupuncture needles. They are often sold in packs of 100 with minimum sizes down to approximately 0.15 mm. However, they can be soft and tricky to use.

Insert the needle into the eraser on a pencil or use a cork. Place the shim on a cutting mat, a foam core, or another sturdy material like a phone book or a writing pad. Put the needle in the middle of the shim, and drill by turning the metal sheet around, instead of the needle. This makes it more likely that you will end up with a good round hole.

Drill once, turn the shim over and sand it lightly with very fine sand paper or abrasive cloth, until the material is smooth. Sand the front of the sheet too. After sanding, gently put the needle in the hole and twist it back and forth without pushing. This clears the hole of any trash and burnishes the edges of the hole.

Hold the shim up to the light, and see if the pinhole is round.

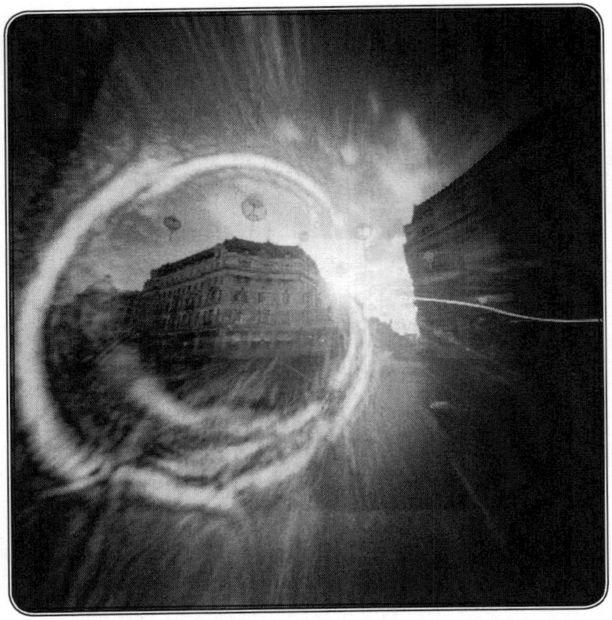

Any deformations may cause diffraction, a type of distortion, caused when light scatters and bends around the edges of the hole, giving you unexpected results.

For our purposes, we'll make the hole as perfect as possible. If you don't trust your eyes there are a number of ways to check if your pinhole is round.

- Use a magnifying glass
- Use an enlarger to view the circle of light
- Scan the sheet and view it at the highest resolution on your computer monitor

You may decide to keep the pinhole rough (right) in order to take advantage of the diffracted light as in this example (above).

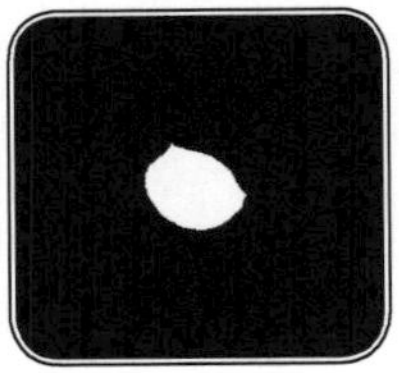

Once it is scanned, open the image in Photoshop or Photoshop Elements and use the Measure Tool to find out the size.

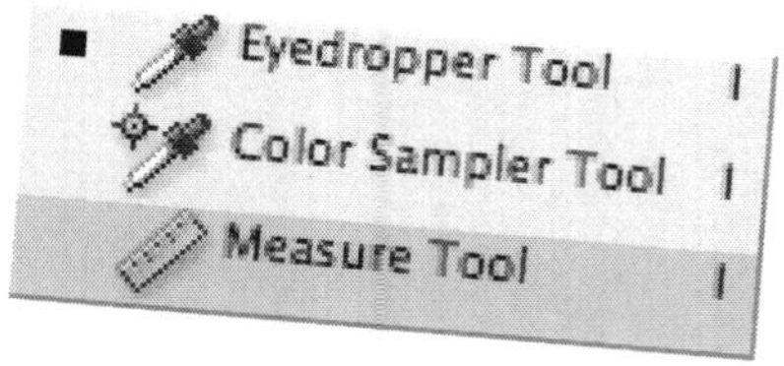

Size matters!

There is an optimum relation between the sharpness of an image, the focal length of the camera, and the size of the pinhole.

The aperture controls the amount of light that reaches the paper. In pinhole cameras the aperture is the size of the hole. A bigger hole needs less exposure time. But a hole that is too large will create a softer, blurry image or even overexposure.

What size pinhole will work with your camera? There are several complicated formulas around, worked out by pinhole-interested scientists, all of which give us more or less the same answers. Many pinholers use the formulas, whilst others simply test their way to finding the right pinhole for their camera.

The ideal hole size

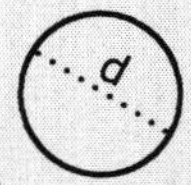

If you know the focal length of your camera you can easily find out the best pinhole size, and your camera's f-stop. The diameter is the length from one side of the hole to the other.

Measured in millimeters

The camera's focal length	Optimum diameter of pinhole	F-stop (and nearest standard f-stop)
10	0.117	85 (90)
20	0.166	121 (128)
30	0.203	148 (128)
40	0.235	171 (180)
50	0.262	191 (180)
60	0.287	209 (180)
70	0.310	226 (256)
80	0.332	241 (256)
90	0.352	256 (256)
100	0.371	270 (256)
150	0.454	330 (360)
200	0.524	381 (360)
250	0.586	426 (360)
300	0.642	467 (512)
350	0.694	505 (512)
400	0.742	539 (512)
450	0.787	572 (512)
500	0.829	603 (512)

Measured in inches

The camera's focal length	Optimum diameter of pinhole	F-stop (and nearest standard f-stop)
0.5	0.0052	96 (90)
1	0.0074	136 (128)
2	0.0104	192 (180)
3	0.0127	235 (256)
4	0.0147	272 (256)
5	0.0165	304 (256)
6	0.0180	333 (360)
7	0.0195	360 (360)
8	0.0208	384 (360)
9	0.0221	408 (360)
10	0.0233	430 (360)
11	0.0244	451 (512)
12	0.0255	471 (512)
13	0.0265	490 (512)
14	0.0275	509 (512)
15	0.0285	526 (512)
16	0.0294	544 (512)
17	0.0303	560 (512)
18	0.0312	577 (512)
19	0.0321	592 (512)
20	0.0329	608 (512)

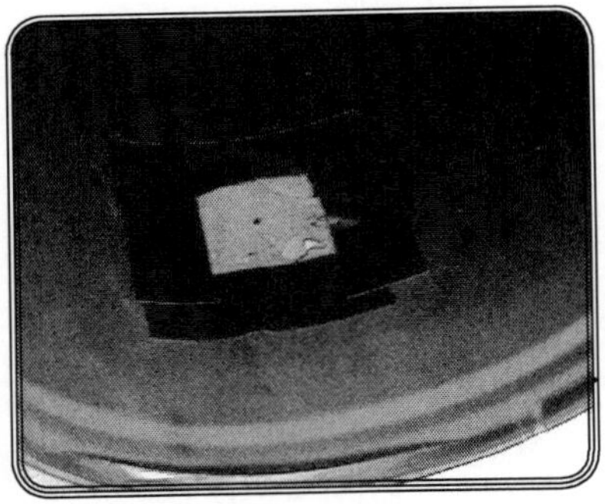

Step 5. Mounting the pinhole

Now that you have produced a decent hole, let's get back to the can. Use the black tape to fasten your pinhole into place. Be certain to center it.

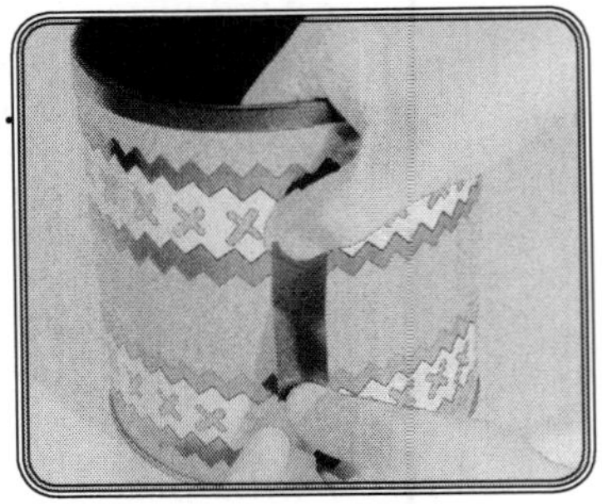

Make a simple shutter using a piece of black tape. Test your camera with the shutter in place.

Step 6. Loading the paper & testing for leaks

Load your camera in the darkroom, with room lights turned off and safelight turned on. The safelight will not harm your photo paper, but the room lights will. Slide your paper into the slots.

Close and seal your camera like you will do later on, when you take a photograph. Expose the camera to bright light for fifteen minutes *without* opening the shutter.

Take the camera back into the darkroom, unload the paper and develop it normally. If the paper is still white, the camera is light proof. If it has turned grey, black or has streaks of black, the camera most probably has a light leak. Find the leak and light proof it with lots of black tape - the pinholer's best friend. Use black photographic tape if possible, it is superior to other types of tape.

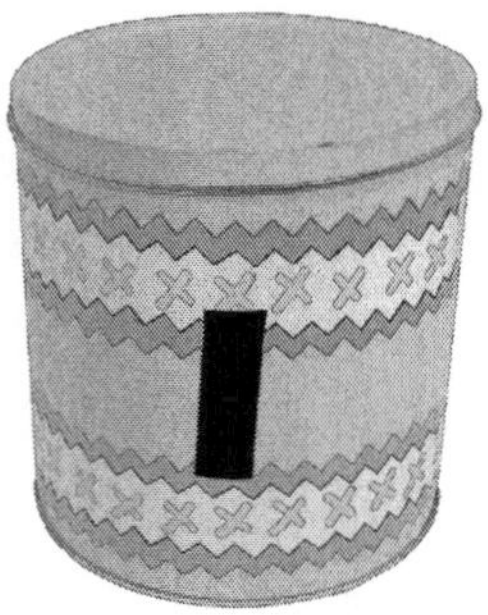

Keep testing and taping until the paper comes out unexposed and white. Once you have got a pure white sheet, you are ready to start making pinhole photographs.

Load your camera. Close the lid and take a picture with your pinhole camera!

Making an advanced shutter

ALTERNATIVEPHOTOGRAPHY.COM conducted a large survey among pinhole photographers. The one thing that made them sweat and swear the most was how to make the perfect shutter.

Don't feel limited, shutters can be as elaborate as your camera. If you are feeling adventurous, experiment your way to a unique shutter. Below are a few tips on how to make an advanced shutter.

Black tape shutter

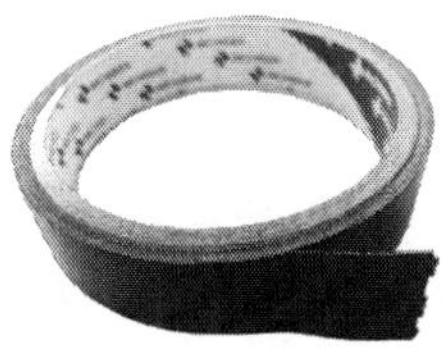

The simplest way possible to make a shutter is to use black tape. Photographic tape is superior to the other varieties, but many pinholers still use electrician's tape, and are happy with this. Aluminium tape can also be used, it is light tight, and is easily torn to the right size. It can be found in building supply stores.

Test your camera with the shutter in place. Once the glue does not stick properly, just replace the old tape for a fresh piece.

Bumper sticker shutter

If your pinhole camera is made from a metal can, and is magnetic, a fridge magnet or a bumper sticker can be used as a simple shutter. Just make sure the magnet is flexible enough to cover the hole, fastens tightly to the can, and that the magnet is a strong one. Genius!

Three plate shutter

If you feel like taking an adventurous detour, see the instructions on the next page. You can use thin plywood or thick cardboard as sturdy and durable base materials.

Optional advanced shutter

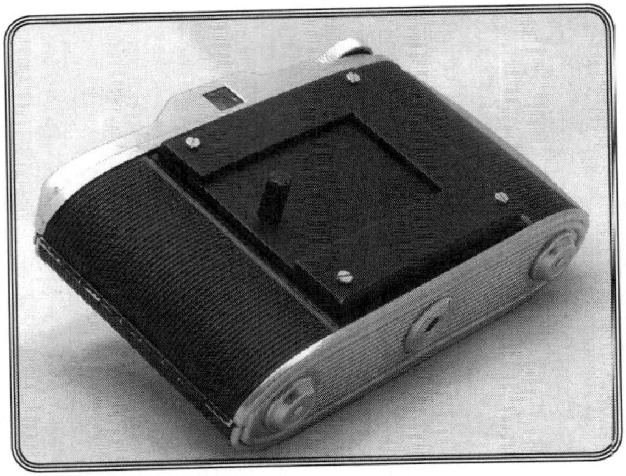

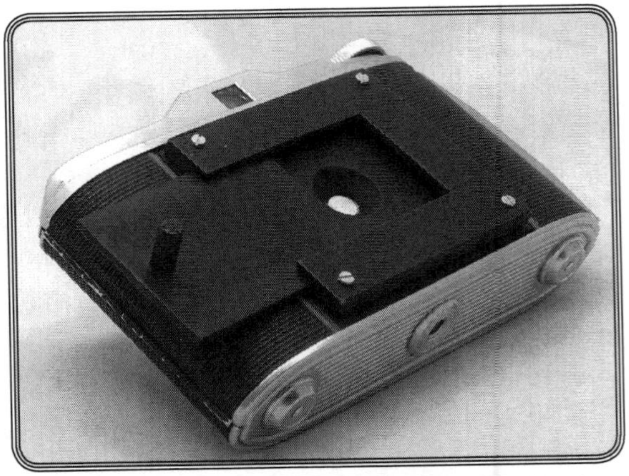

1. The bottom plate

The bottom plate covers the opening of the camera. It also has a hole which is drilled and countersunk where the pinhole plate is placed. The hole should be wide enough to avoid creating a vignette.

2. The middle and shutter plate

The shutter plate should fit tightly into the middle plate, but still be able to slide.

3. The top plate

Use screws to mount the top plate, which will hold the shutter and the other two plates in place.

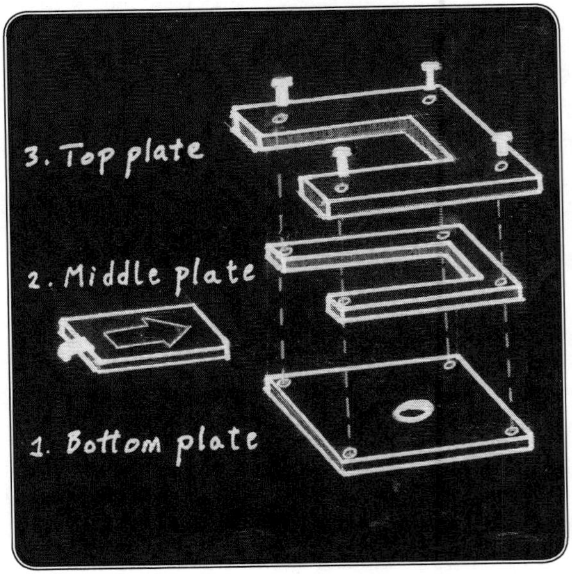

Shutter on the camera above by Lena Källberg.

Taking the picture

YOUR CAMERA IS READY, loaded with photographic paper and you have found the perfect scene. You have got a light tight shutter, but how long do you open it?

There is a perfect exposure time and it depends on your camera, the film you are using, the size of your pinhole and the amount of light available. If you don't expose it long enough your negative will be too light and if you leave it too long your negative will turn too dark.

There are two basic methods you can use to determine exposure – use a light meter and do a calculation, or test your way to good results. You will find that it is probably the latter or a combination of these two that will work for you.

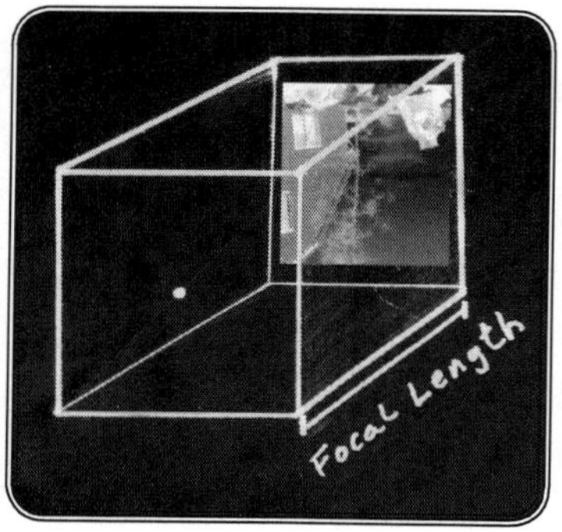

The focal length of your pinhole camera is the distance between the pinhole and the paper or film you have loaded the camera with.

Keep notes of your exposure times and the results you get. Learn from your experiences.

Doing the math

$$\frac{\text{focal length}}{\text{diameter of pinhole}} = \text{f-stop}$$

F-stops

If you know the size of the pinhole and the focal length you can work out the f-stop of your camera. The f-stop will help you work out the right exposure time.

The formula for calculating the f-stop of your camera is the focal length divided by the size of diameter of the pinhole.

F-stops have a 'standard sequence'. If you have an ordinary camera, you can see the f-numbers on the lens.

The f-stop sequence

Ordinary lenses rarely go beyond f/22. The sequence is:

f/16	f/180
f/22	f/256
f/32	f/360
f/45	f/512
f/64	f/720
f/90	f/1024
f/128	

Measuring light intensity for a pinhole camera

Here is how to determine exposure time with a light meter.

In a perfect world, when you know the f-stop of your pinhole camera you set the light meter to an f-stop which is the same as your camera and take a reading.

A digital or ordinary camera with a built in light meter can also work if it has a manual setting. Keep the ISO and f-stop constant and read the shutter speed.

An ordinary camera's f-stops may vary from between f/3.5 to f/22 which allows for very short exposure times. Pinhole cameras tend to have f-stops of somewhere between f/200 and f/500 which means exposure times are considerably longer.

To simplify exposure you could say that each f-stop doubles or halves the time you need to keep the shutter open - this is known as the law of reciprocity*. If you change the pinhole size you have to increase or decrease exposure times accordingly.

Working out exposure time with a light meter

Let's assume that your pinhole camera's f-stop is close to 256 and your light meter is set at f/22. The light meter takes a reading of 0.5 seconds at f/22. You then double the exposure time with each f-stop so that the correct exposure for:

f/22 = 0.5 seconds
f/32 = 1 second
f/45 = 2 seconds
f/64 = 4 seconds
f/90 = 8 seconds
f/128 = 16 seconds
f/180 = 32 seconds
f/256 = 64 seconds.

In our case with a pinhole camera that has an f-stop of close to 256 we can say that 64 seconds exposure time would be a good starting point.

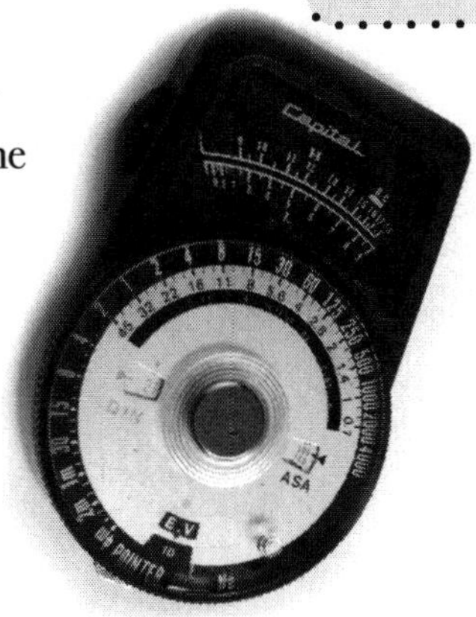

*Note: The law of reciprocity determines the exposure of film or paper. The exposure is the intensity of the light times the time the material is exposed. If the light is more intense, the time can be reduced, or if it is cloudy, the time has to be increased.

If you don't have a light meter try this exposure table

The table below will give you approximate exposure times. If your first print comes out too dark when you have developed it, shorten the exposure time. If the image is too light, then increase the exposure time.

The exposure table assumes you are using black & white photographic paper in your pinhole camera. Film is more sensitive and needs much shorter exposure times than photographic paper.

Exposure table - a starting point

	Weather	**F-stop of your pinhole camera**				
		128	180	256	360	512
	Bright sunshine	15 s	30 s	60 s	1.5-3 min	3-6 min
	Hazy sunshine	30 s	1-2 min	3-5 min	5-10 min	15-45 min
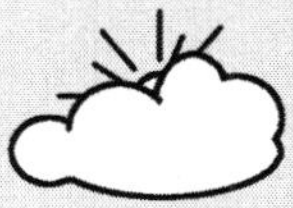	Cloudy but bright	60 s	2-4 min	6-10 min	10-20 min	30-90 min
	Cloudy	2-4 min	4-8 min	15-30 min	30-60 min	1.5 h-3 h

If you are taking photographs indoors with your pinhole camera, you can use the "Cloudy" exposure time and double it as a starting point.

Camera movement

Place the camera on a flat solid surface. Secure it in place even if there is no wind. It is best not to hold the camera in your hands unless you are after a 'blurry' effect.

Law of reciprocity failure

WHEN LIGHT INTENSITY is extremely low, for example, in nightscape photography, or exposure times are very long, as in pinhole cameras sometimes the reciprocity law doesn't apply.

You will have to compensate by adjusting exposure times.

A rough guide on how to compensate for the reciprocity law failure and achieve the required exposure on your print is provided in the table.

Reciprocity law failure compensation table

Metered exposure time	Reciprocity failure compensation - multiply your metered exposure time with this number	Actual exposure time you should use when taking the photograph
1 second	x 1.25	1.25 s
5 seconds	x 1.5	7.5 s
15 seconds	x 2	30 s
45 seconds	x 2.5	112 s
2 minutes	x 3	6 minutes
5 minutes	x 4	20 minutes
10 minutes	x 5	50 minutes
20 minutes	x 6	2 hours
30 minutes	x 7	3.5 hours
40 minutes	x 8	5.5 hours

Different photographic materials

Start with black & white photographic printing paper. It is easy to handle. It can be loaded easily with a red safelight and it is easy to develop yourself.

Once you've got the knack of pinholing, move on to medium format film, standard 35 mm black & white film, color film, large sheet film, color papers or even liquid emulsion.

Liquid emulsion is a photographic emulsion used to coat various materials such as cloth or textured paper. It can then be used in a pinhole camera.

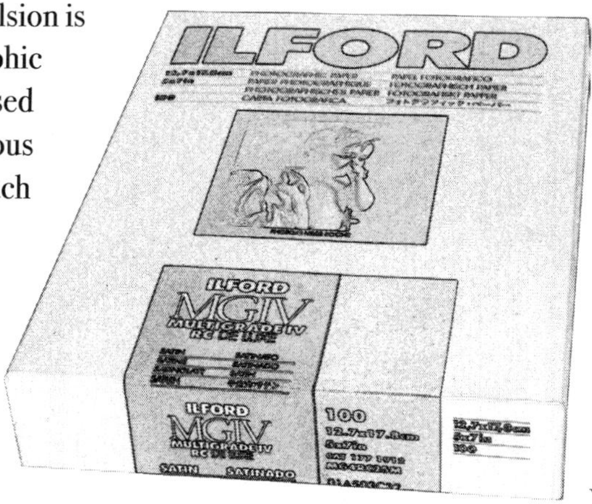

Try infrared film, which captures infrared light, not normally visible to the human eye.

Experienced pinholers often use film so that they have a master copy of their pinhole image which can be reproduced in multiple ways.

Paper

Photographic paper is coated with an emulsion that consists of gelatin and silver halides. The gelatin is transparent and holds the silver halides in place during the exposure. The gelatin also allows chemicals to reach all the grains during processing.

You can buy papers in any well-stocked camera store or on the Internet. Papers are manufactured in a number of sizes, some common ones are:

Inches	Centimeter
5x7	12.7x17.8
8x10	20.3x25.4
11x14	27.9x35.6
12x16*	30.5x40.6
16x20	40.6x50.8
20x24	50.8x61

You may want to decide which size paper you will be using *before* making your camera. If your camera needs smaller paper or has another shape there is nothing stopping you from taking a pair of scissors and cutting the paper to the size or shape you want. Just make sure to do this in the darkroom with the safelight on!

Note: *12x16 is not a standard size in USA.

Types of paper

THE TWO MOST COMMON types of paper are Resin Coated (RC) and Fiber Based (FB).

Resin Coated paper has a thin plastic layer, or coating on both sides of the paper base, a resin coat. It seals the paper and makes washing and drying stages considerably shorter than for Fiber Based paper. It tends to stay flatter than Fiber Based papers. On the other hand the archival qualities of Resin Coated papers are not as good as the Fiber Based ones.

Fiber Based papers consists of a paper base coated with a baryta*. It will absorb the chemicals into the core of the paper. Longer washing times are required, and they should also be air-dried. They are generally easier to retouch and hand color and have a longer lifespan than Resin Coated papers.

*Barium sulfate, a white crystalline solid, insoluble in water

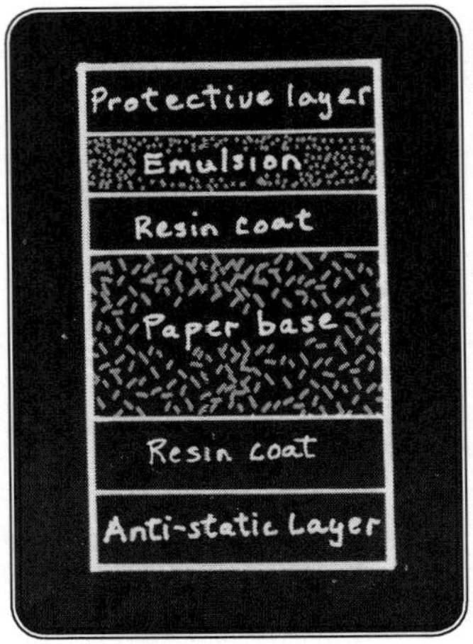

The different layers of a Resin Coated paper.

Which type of paper should I start with?

Start with a Resin Coated paper with a semi-mat surface. Experiment with other papers once you have a few pinholes under your belt.

Glossy or Mat?

Mat (also called matt and matte) papers are usually considered better for pinholing than glossy surfaces because gloss can cause reflection inside the camera.

A mat surface diffuses light and the print appears equally bright from whichever angle it is viewed. But a mat surface may have a shorter tonal range than a glossy one. Very confusingly Ilford call their mat papers 'satin'. So, if you want a mat Ilford paper, get the box marked 'satin'.

If you prefer the shiny surfaces of a glossy paper, you can print your pinhole onto a glossy paper when you turn your negative image into a positive. This is done by contact printing at the end of the developing process.

Film

Film has several advantages over paper. It is more light sensitive, and it is easier to reproduce and enlarge images from film. You can also create a winding mechanism in your camera and take several photos before needing to reload.

Film often has a higher tolerance to exposure mistakes. A paper negative doesn't allow a lot of room for adjusting in the darkroom.

Because it can be difficult to determine exposure times when pinholing it is an advantage to have flexibility when creating prints.

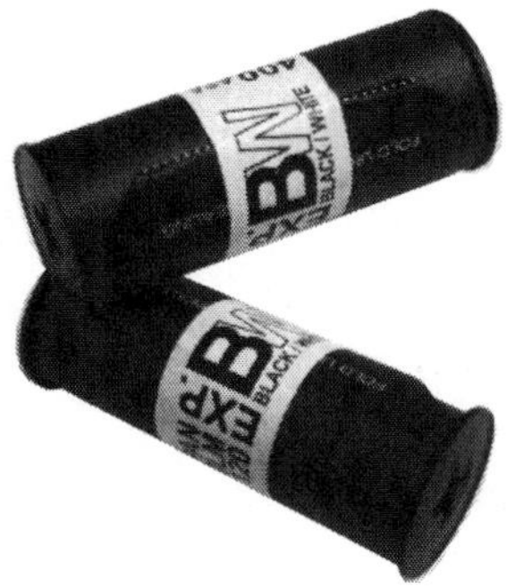

Color film

Color film will enrich your pinhole experience. Colors often shift during relatively long exposure times yielding unexpected color twists in your final image.

Try combining an uneven pinhole with color film to create scattered light effects. Suddenly you may have rainbows around your subjects.

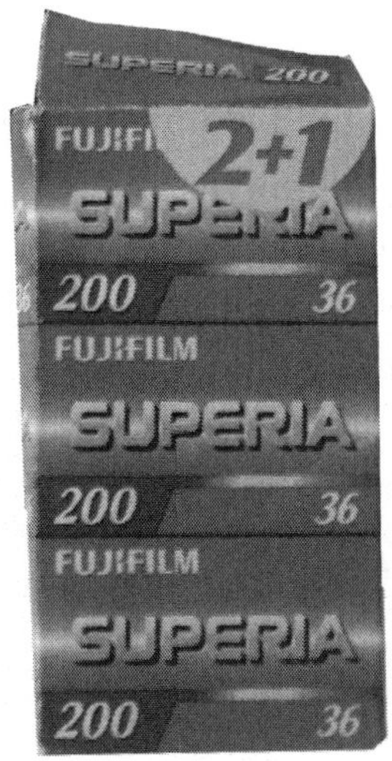

Setting up a darkroom

THE SKILLS NEEDED to develop a photograph are easy to learn. And you don't need a lot of equipment to create your own darkroom.

Any room that can be made light tight, such as a bathroom or cupboard, can be used as a darkroom. It is ideal to have a sink with running water, but not essential. Final washing can be done in daylight.

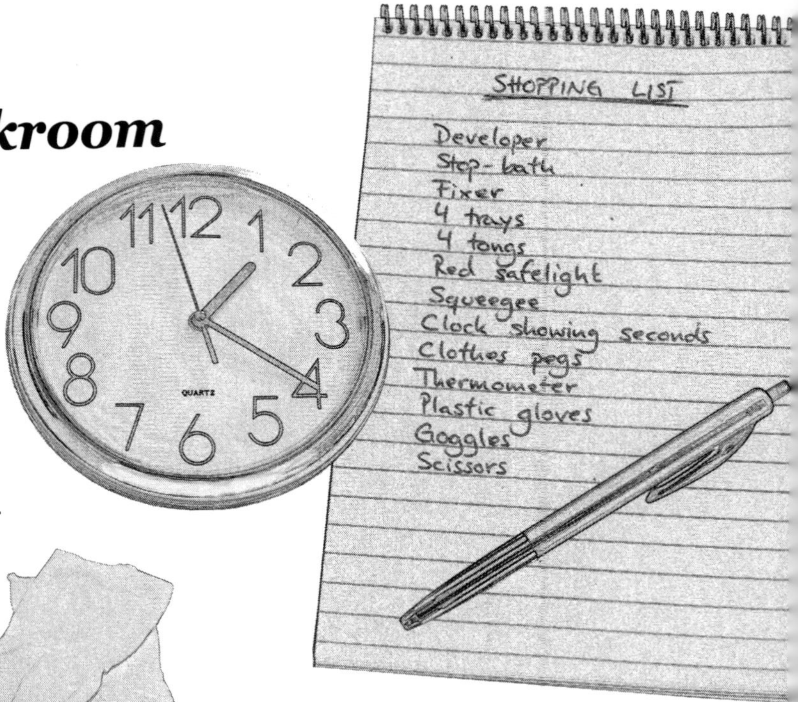

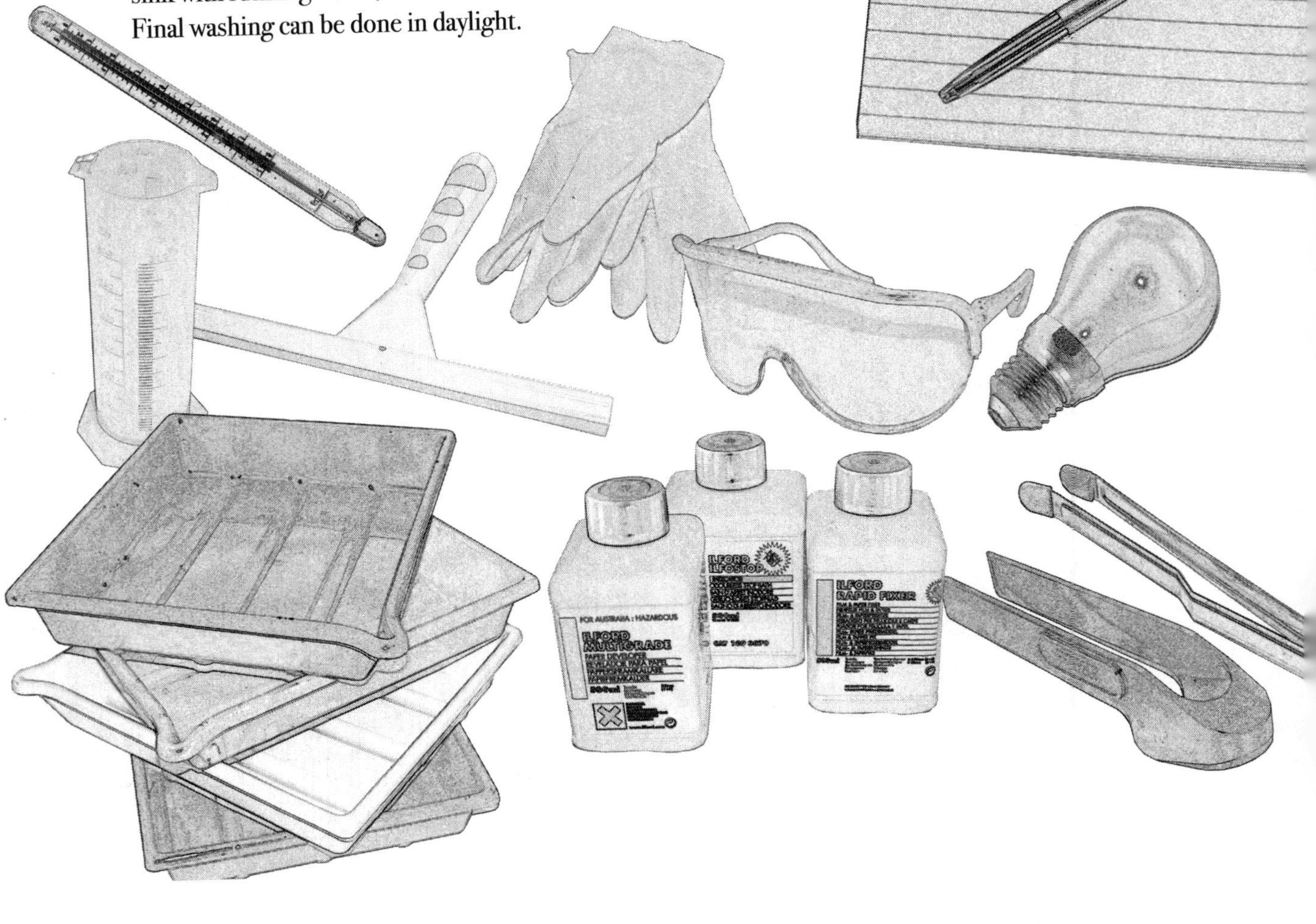

Organizing the workspace

Whatever the shape or size of the room, it is important to make it as orderly as possible. You will be working in a very dimly lit room and handling chemicals at the same time. Organization minimizes accidents.

You can set everything up with the room lights turned on. Ordinary room light is not harmful to the chemicals. Just make sure your photographic papers are in a light proof box.

Arrange the workspace so that the trays can be put out in sequence. Start with the developing tray, then the stop-bath, followed by the fixer. Finish up in the sink or wash area.

Tip! Do a darkroom test: Is your darkroom light proof?

- Take out a piece of unexposed photographic paper and place it, shiny side up, in the same position where the developing trays will sit.
- Cover half the paper with a piece of cardboard and wait a few minutes.
- Process the paper as if it were an ordinary photograph.
- Switch on the light. If the paper is still white as snow, then your darkroom passed the test. If you see any shading of grey on the side of the paper that was not covered by cardboard, then your darkroom is leaking too much light, and this may affect your prints. Light proof it!

Safety precautions

Photographic chemicals must be used correctly. Follow the health and safety recommendations on the packaging and use common sense.

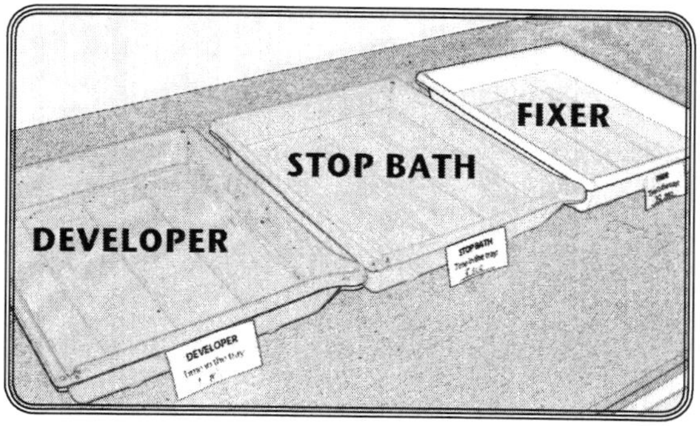

Developing the picture

For many photographers, making a print is its own form of art. The darkroom is where the developing process can be refined. It is where the picture comes to life. It can be made lighter or darker, finer or sharper. These techniques will come with experience.

Start processing

Switch the safelight on and get started. There are five basic steps to processing an image:

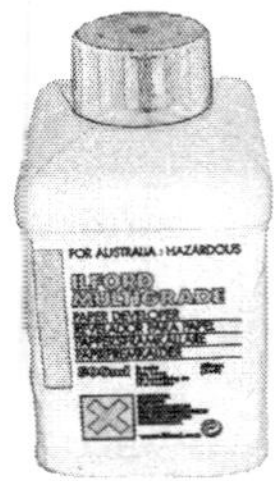

Step 1. Developer – Making the image visible

When the shutter was opened, the silver crystals in the emulsion were exposed to light. When the paper is placed in the developer tray, the chemicals of the developer convert those crystals into metallic silver, and the image appears.

- Set the clock or timer and start it when you are ready.
- Slide the paper, emulsion side down, into the developing tray. Press it down with the tongs. It is important to use tongs dedicated to each tray, or the chemicals will be contaminated.
- Turn the paper over so you can see the developing image. The image will start to appear after about 10 seconds. If the paper floats up, push it back into the chemicals with the tongs.
- Agitate the solution by rocking the tray gently.
- When the time stated by the chemical manufacturer is up, the print should be fully developed.

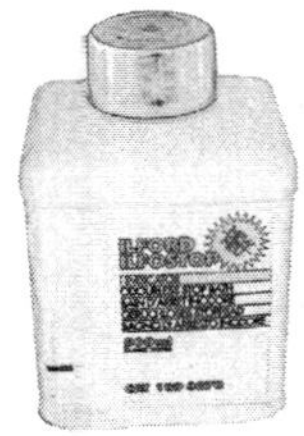

Step 2. Stop bath – Stops the image developing

The stop bath is a chemical solution that rapidly halts the action of the developer.

- Transfer the print to the stop bath.
- Pick up the tongs dedicated to the stop bath.
- Keep the print fully immersed while rocking the tray.
- Lift the print out of the stop bath and hold it up to drain any excess chemicals.
- Transfer the print to the tray with the fixer.

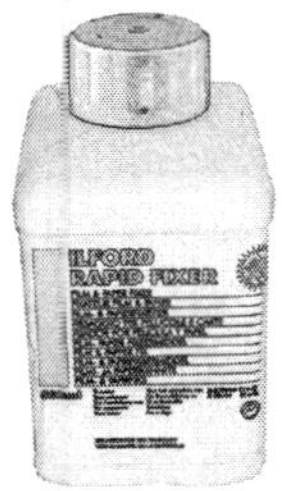

Step 3. Fixer – Stabilizes the image

The fixer dissolves any leftover emulsion, removing undeveloped and unexposed crystals that otherwise would darken the image.

- Submerge the print into the fixer and pick up the tongs dedicated to the fixer.
- Keep the print fully immersed in the fixer for the time required.
- Agitate, or rock the tray slowly.
- Lift the print out of the fixer and transfer it to the water for cleaning.

Step 4. Washing – To clean the image

After the fixer you can turn on the room light and examine your print.

Wash away any leftover chemicals that may otherwise harm the final photograph. Use running water for 2 minutes, if using Resin Coated paper. Make sure the print moves around and doesn't get stuck at the bottom of the tray.

Step 5. Drying the image

Dry the image on a flat surface or hang on a line with clothes pegs.

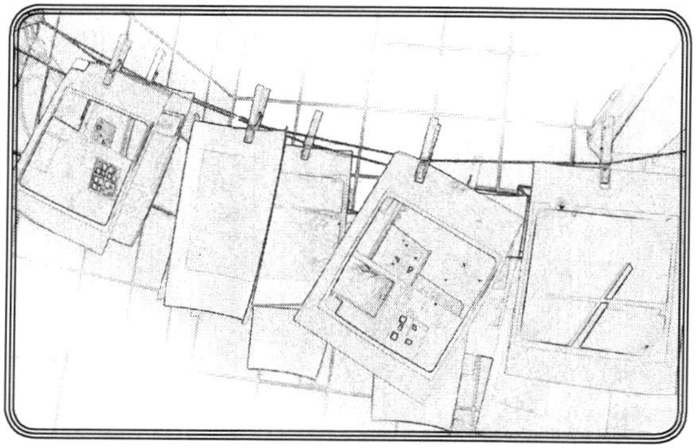

"I know few things in the range of science more surprising than the gradual appearance of the picture on a blank sheet, especially the first time the experiment is witnessed."

Henry Fox Talbot

Time in the tray

The instructions here are the times that your photograph should be in each tray when using Ilford chemicals and Ilford paper. For any other brand, check the times, and temperatures on the bottles:

Developer: Ilford "Multigrade"
Dilution: 1+9 (1 part developer, 9 water)
Time in tray: 1 minute
Temperature: 20 C / 68 F

Stop bath: Ilford "Ilfostop"
Dilution: 1+19 (1 part stop bath, 19 water)
Time in tray: 10 seconds
Temperature: 18-24 C / 64-75 F

Fixer: Ilford "Rapid"
Dilution: 1+4 (1 part fixer, 4 water)
Time in tray: 30 seconds
Temperature: 18-24 C / 64-75 F

Wash: In running tap water
Resin coated paper:
Temperature: Above 5 C / 41 F
Time: 2 minutes minimum and no longer than 15 minutes
Fibre based paper:
Temperature: Above 5 C / 41 F
Time: 60 minutes

The above washing temperatures are recommendations from Ilford using Ilford chemicals and photo papers, the usual praxis is to keep the water temperature between 18-27 C / 65-75 F.

Turn the negative into a positive by contact printing

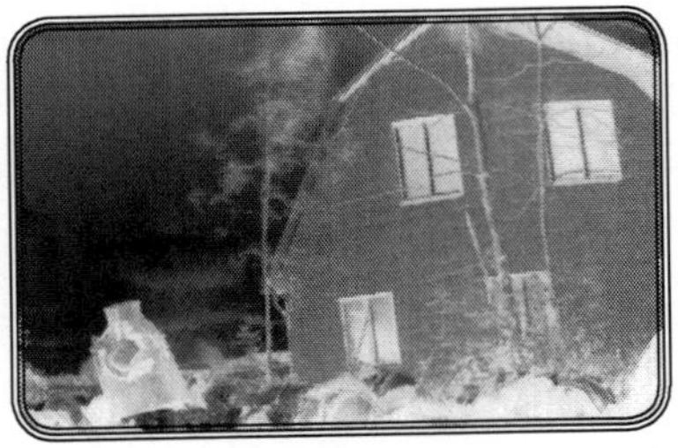

Above is a negative and to the right, the same image turned into a positive print.

YOU NOW HAVE an image in which light areas appear dark, and dark areas are light - a negative. You can easily turn it into a positive in the darkroom by contact printing. You don't even have to wait for the print to dry. Wet and dry contact printing basically use the same method:

First, make sure the photo paper does not have a logo or any text on the back. This will show through, and be embedded into the print.

1. **TURN LIGHTS OFF** and red safelight on.

2. **FETCH A FRESH PHOTO PAPER.** Close the box carefully, the lights will go on soon! If you are using the wet method, dip the unexposed paper in the water too.

3. **MAKE A SANDWICH** from a clean, flat and sturdy board, the unexposed paper, emulsion side UP, the paper negative, emulsion side DOWN – that is the side with the print on it, and a piece of glass. Press them together. If your papers are wet, squeegee any excess water out first.

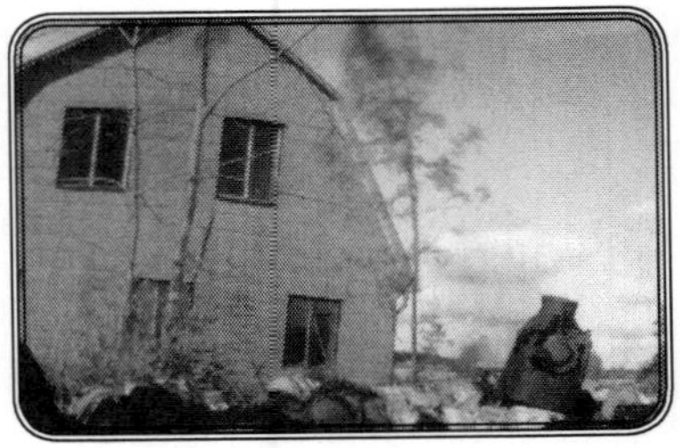

4. **TURN THE ROOM LIGHT ON** for 2-3 seconds.

5. **DEVELOP YOUR POSITIVE** print normally, safelight on. You now have both a positive and a negative print of the same image. You can of course make several more prints if you are happy with the result.

For the positive print, you can use the same paper you used in your pinhole camera, or take the opportunity to switch to a glossy or Fibre Based paper if you prefer.

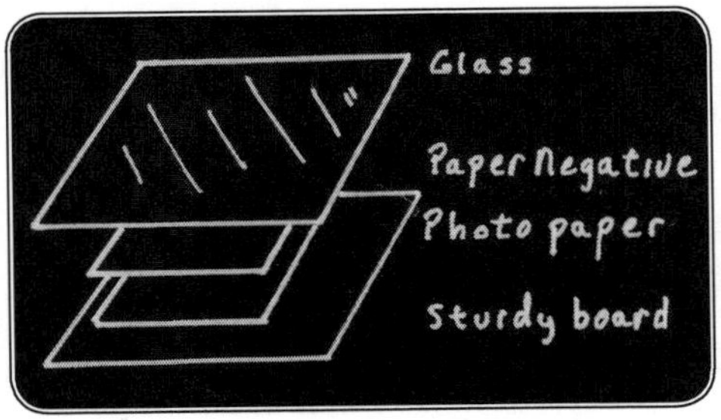

Another way to make a positive is to scan it into your computer and use a program such as Photoshop or The Gimp - which is free - to invert and adjust it.

Trouble shooting

All that came out is just a white sheet of paper!

- You may have inserted the paper back to front in the camera. Make sure the shiny side, which has the emulsion on it, is facing the hole.

My negative is too light!

- Was the exposure time too short? Try extending it, by about double the time.

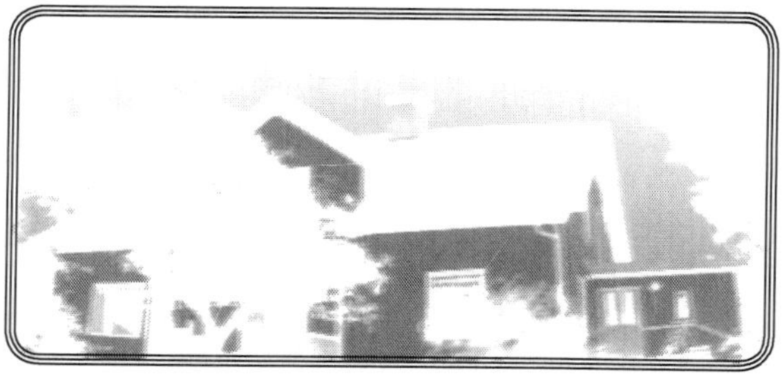

My negative is too dark!

- Was the camera pointed straight at the sun during exposure?
- Was the exposure too long? Try shortening it, by about half the time.
- Your camera may have a light leak. Check the camera for leaks as described earlier.

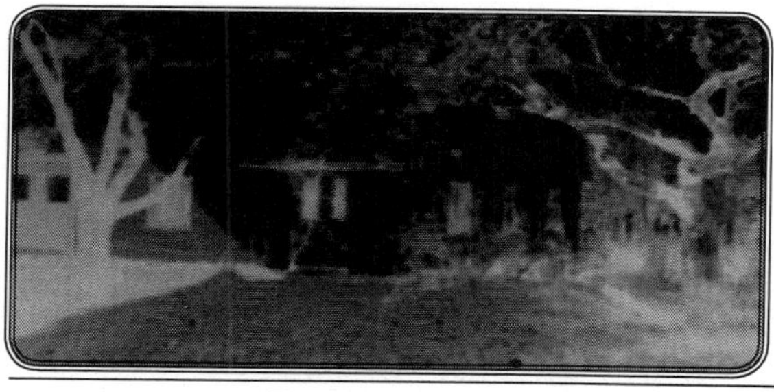

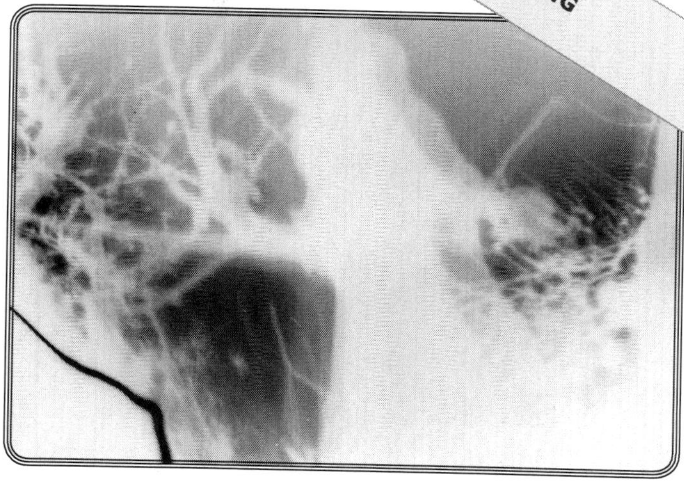

My negative is blurry!

- Is the pinhole in your camera too large? If so, all photographs you take with it will come out blurry. Try making a new, smaller pinhole.
- Did the camera move during exposure? Double check that it is on a flat surface and that it is steady.
- Is the subject that you are trying to take a picture of moving?

Pinhole artists and their special cameras

NOW THAT YOU have made your first pinhole camera, taken your first pictures and truly entered the world of the pinhole, we hope that you are eager for more. The following inspiring pages can give you an idea of what can be done with more advanced pinhole cameras. The following artists have worked with pinholing, and perhaps also other processes, for several years. Many of them are renowned in their specific field, and many have been exhibited worldwide. Take a look and get inspired.

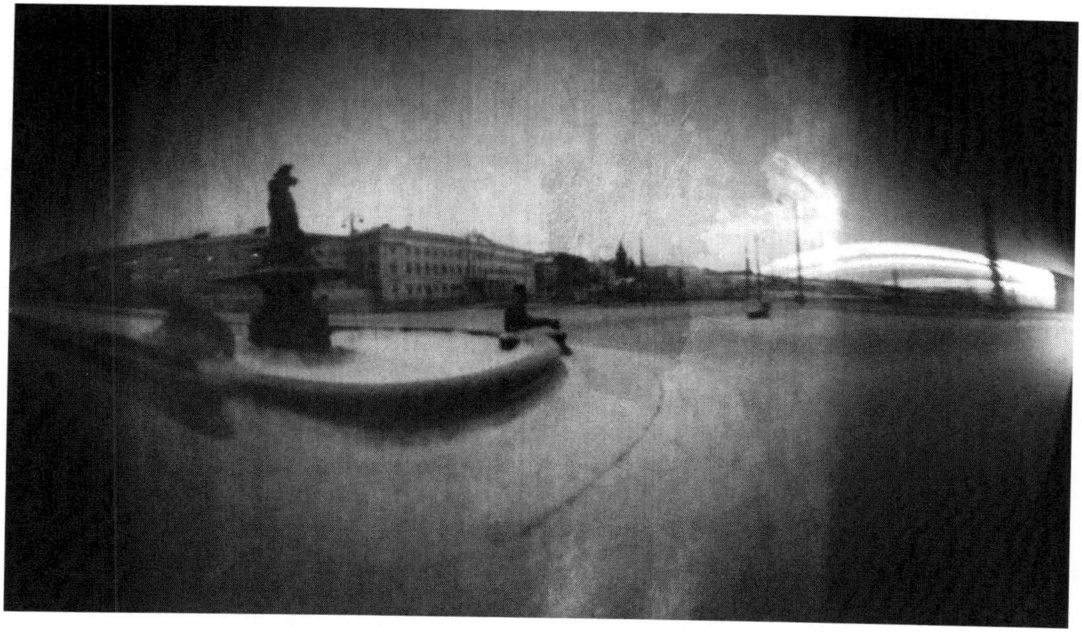

Solargraphics - Extremely long exposure

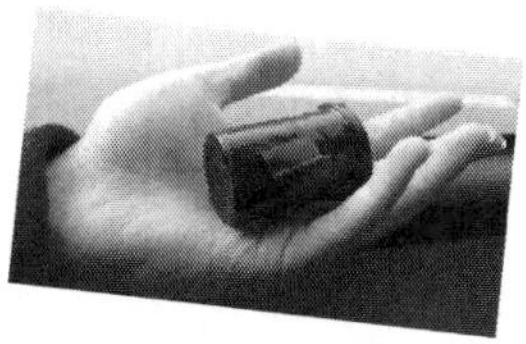

Tarja Trygg *Havis Amanda © 2003*

Simple film canisters map the movement of the sun on a particular horizon, usually between an equinox and a solstice. The image shows up on the overexposed black & white photo paper, in color, without the use of further chemical processes. Magic!

A black film canister houses a piece of black & white photo paper. Black tape covers the pinhole - which is about 0.20 mm. The camera is taped onto a lamppost, a window or a building and left to expose the paper for several months. This is the statue, *Havis Amanda*, in the market place in the heart of Helsinki, Finland. The result is a solargraph. The paths of the sun have been recorded and made visible on the landscape. No chemicals are needed. The paper negative photo is scanned in and inverted into a positive in Photoshop. Levels, contrast, brightness and color balance are adjusted. The original photograph is in color.

www.solargraphy.com

Multiple pinhole - 360 degrees

Jan Kapoor *Oakland Series #1 © 2005*

Six pinholes of the same size in a hexagonal box, with the film wrapped around a cylinder in the middle, create 360 degree images. The hexagonal pinhole camera started out life as a Christmas ornament box. Jan cut openings in each of the six sides, and made pinholes from disposable aluminum cookie sheet. Making six pinholes of the same size was the hardest part. Jan gets a 360 degree image of a single location by leaving the camera in one place and using all six pinholes, simultaneously or individually over time. At other times Jan experiments with exposing through just one or two pinholes, then relocating the camera several more times for additional exposures with the other pinholes. Each of the individual "frames" reverses side-to-side and blends into the adjacent ones, making a completely unpredictable but fascinating image.

The film Jan uses is Arista lith film cut to 6x13 inches, wrapped and taped around the oatmeal box cylinder, glued onto the inside of the lid. After exposure, the film is developed in a very dilute solution of Dektol developer. Jan pushes the processes further, using cyanotype or platinum and palladium to print her images.

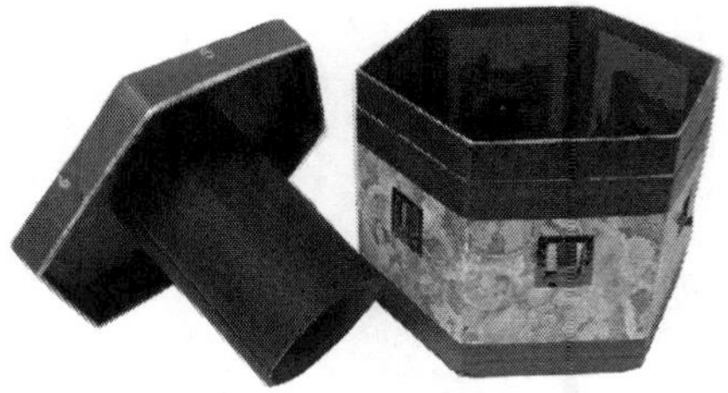

www.jankapoor.net

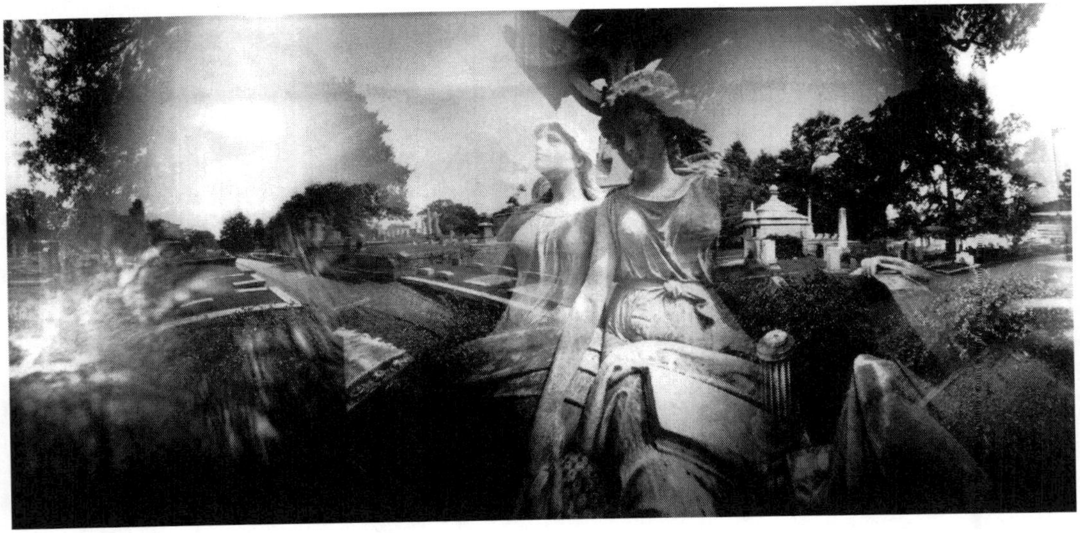

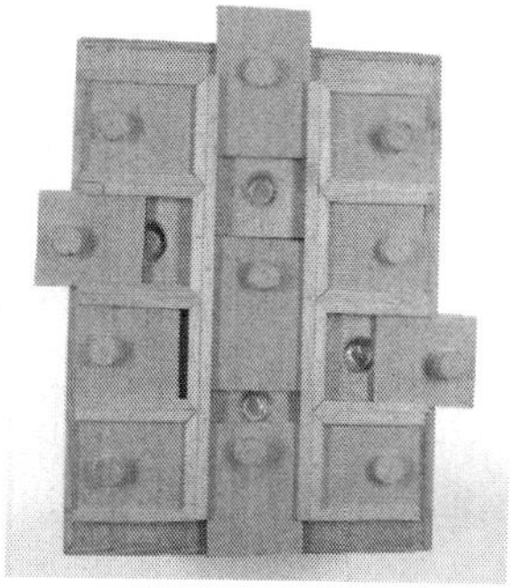

Multipinhole

Thomas Kellner

Dying Nature © 1994

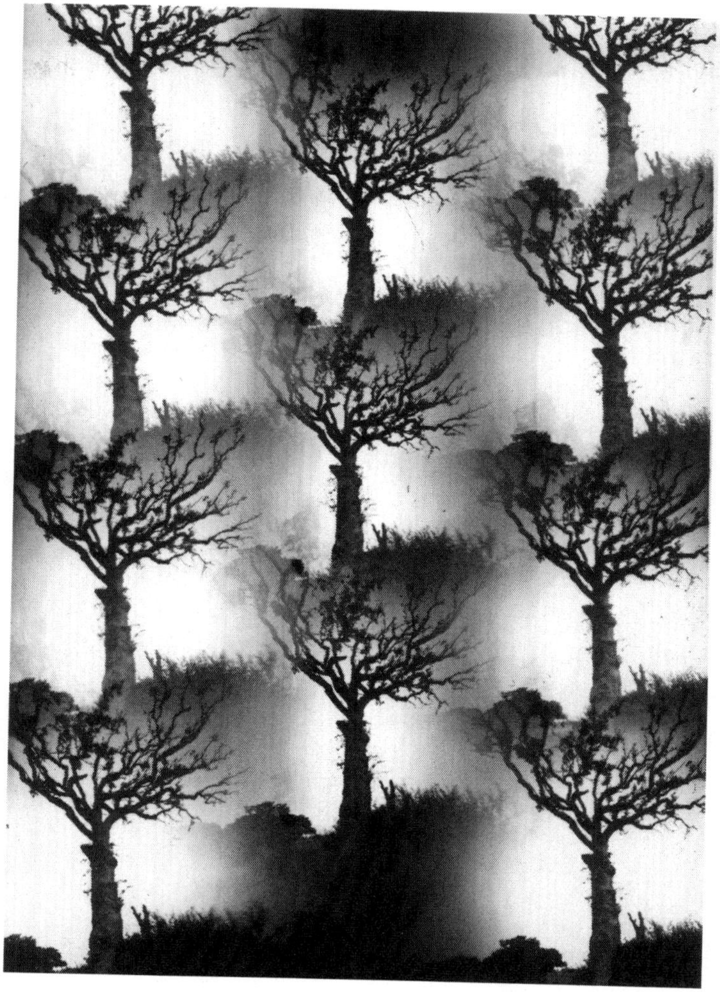

German photographer Thomas Kellner has been widely renowned for his "cubistic" depictions of famous buildings, and has worked extensively with combining multiple images.

In the early 90s Thomas built several multipinhole cameras, in which a single piece of film, fused the image parts almost seamlessly into each other. He even made one camera with as many as 19 exposures on a very long piece of film. The one shown here has eleven holes, placed in a grid.

Each hole has its own shutter and the camera is loaded with a film sheet sized 16.4x23.5 cm (6.4x9.2 inches), from which Thomas makes silver prints or cyanotypes.

www.tkellner.com

Polaroid pinhole camera

Arunas Kulikauskas *Ball © Worldwide Pinhole Photography Day 2007*

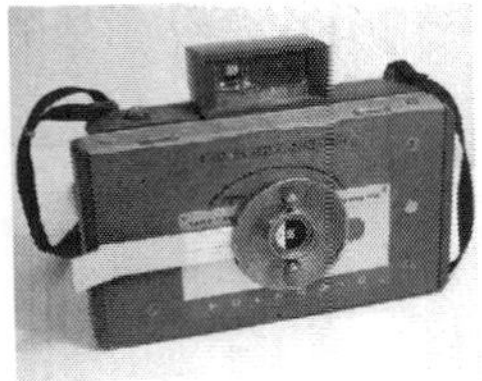

Arunas buys old Polaroid land cameras on eBay, yard sales or flee markets. He strips the film holder from the bellow and lens and attaches it to a cigar box. The thickness of the cigar box determines focal distance. On one side of the box a rectangular opening of the exact size of a Polaroid film holder is made. There is a pinhole on the opposite side of the box.

So far Arunas has made twelve cameras. The camera used here is called Polaroid pinhole camera Churchill, made from a cigar box and Polaroid Automatic 104 land camera back, with a focal length of 33 mm and a pinhole size of 0.22 mm.

www.flickr.com/photos/arunas

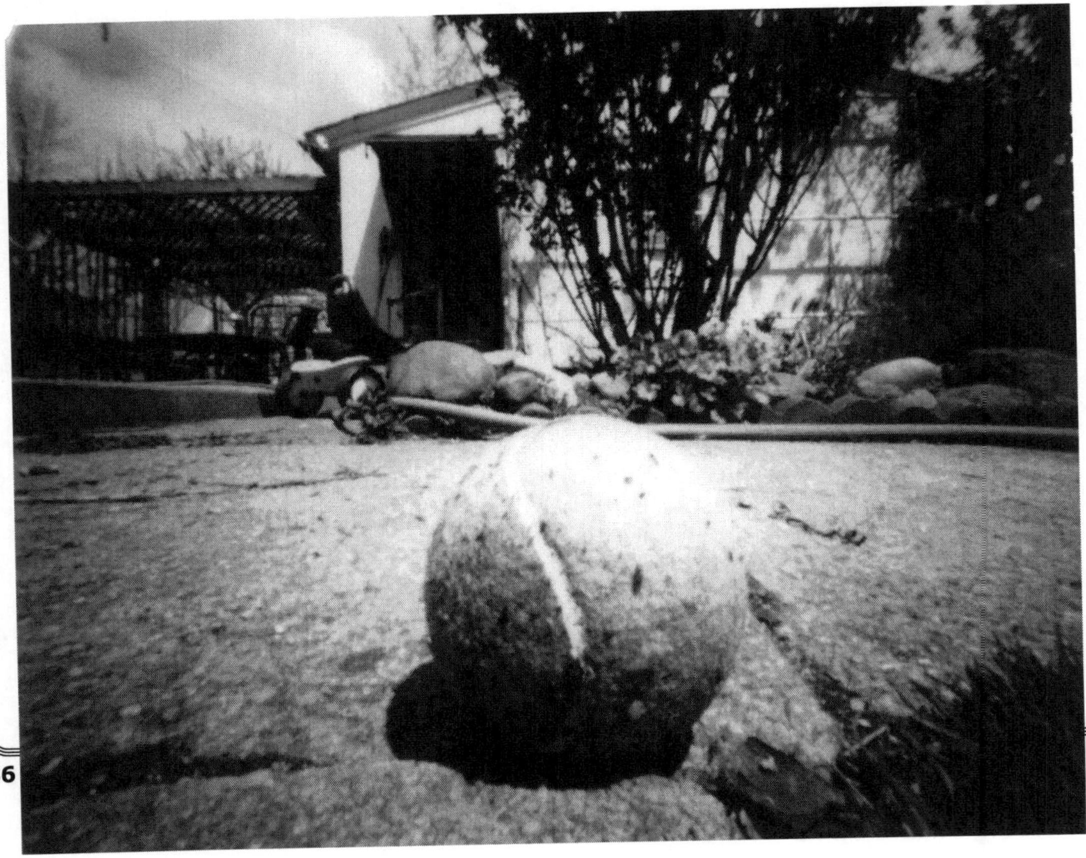

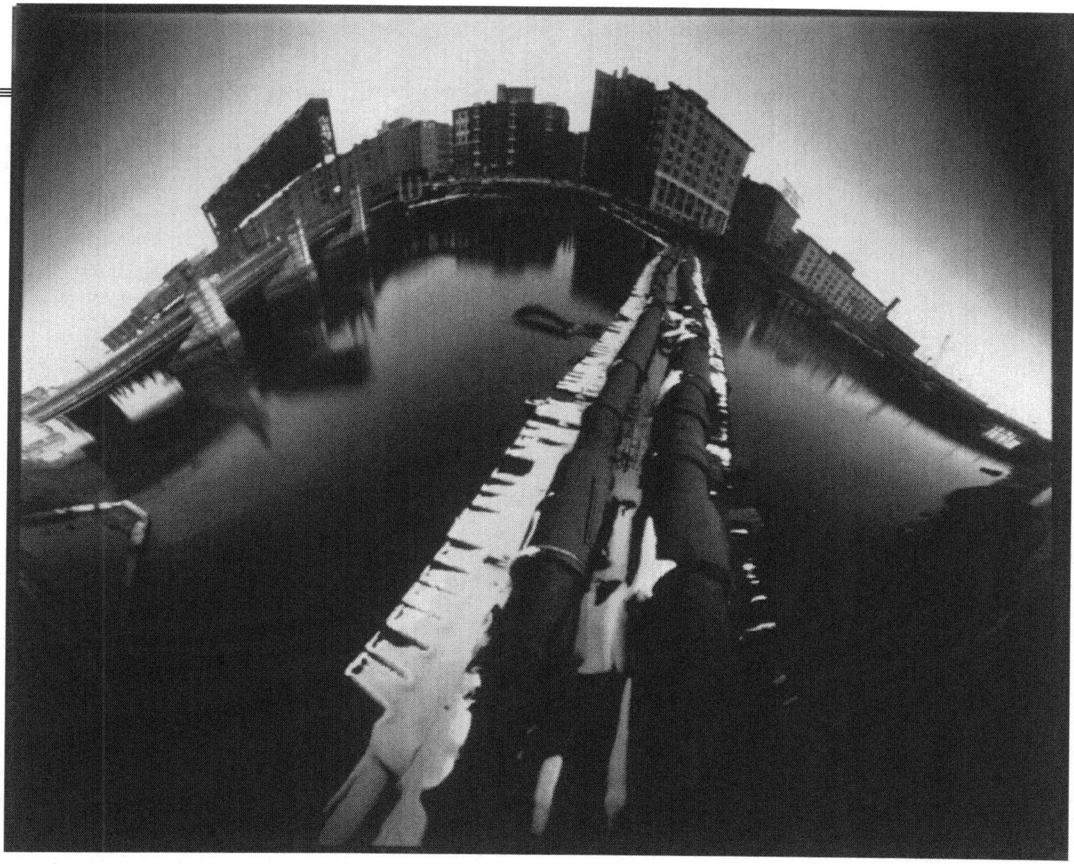

Bent film plane

Walter Crump *Abandoned Conduit © 2002. Part of "The Bent Cities Project"*

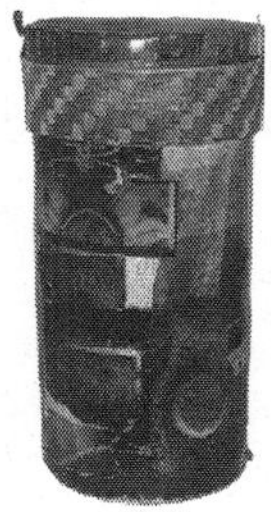

This camera is made from a 10" diameter x 17" Sona tube. A 16x20" paper negative is wrapped around the circumference of the camera. Walter can choose between two pinholes - one in the center of the camera making the horizon appear in the center of the image and one about 1/3 off center placing the horizon either higher or lower.

The photographs are exposed to light after development and before fixing, where Walter "paints" with bleaches, fixer and developer. After fixing, the photographs are bleached, toned and often soaked in a coffee or tea bath.

www.waltercrump.com

Extreme size

Jo Babcock *Cornfield, Upstate New York © 1989*

'By the time I enrolled in college I thought I had my vocation all picked out,' says Jo Babcock. 'I wanted to be a professional photographer. To my surprise, they had placed me in the Art Department. I called them right up and said, "You've made a mistake. I don't want to be an artist. I want to be a photographer!'"

Now, Jo is a photographer and camera creator, best known for his 40x60" VW Van Camera, suitcase cameras, and converting over two hundred recycled objects into pinhole and simple lens cameras.

A pinhole aperture is mounted into the center of the side door and a lens/mirror device is mounted on top of the roof. This gives the option of either making one hour pinhole exposures or six second lens/mirror exposures directly onto photographic paper rolled out across the floor, or tacked to the wall inside the van. In the side of the door there is a hole, and the van is transformed to a pinhole camera.

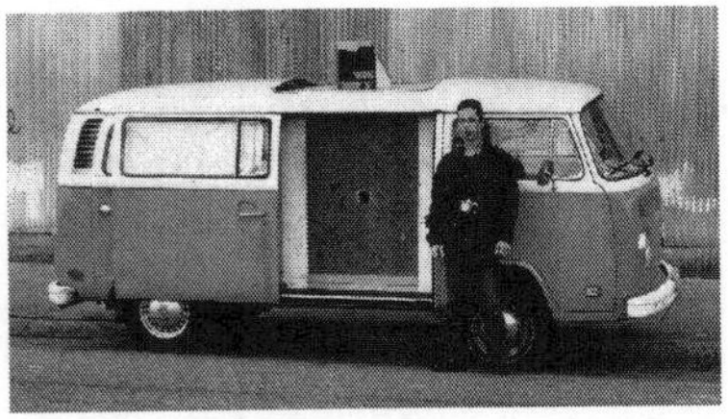

www.jobabcock.com

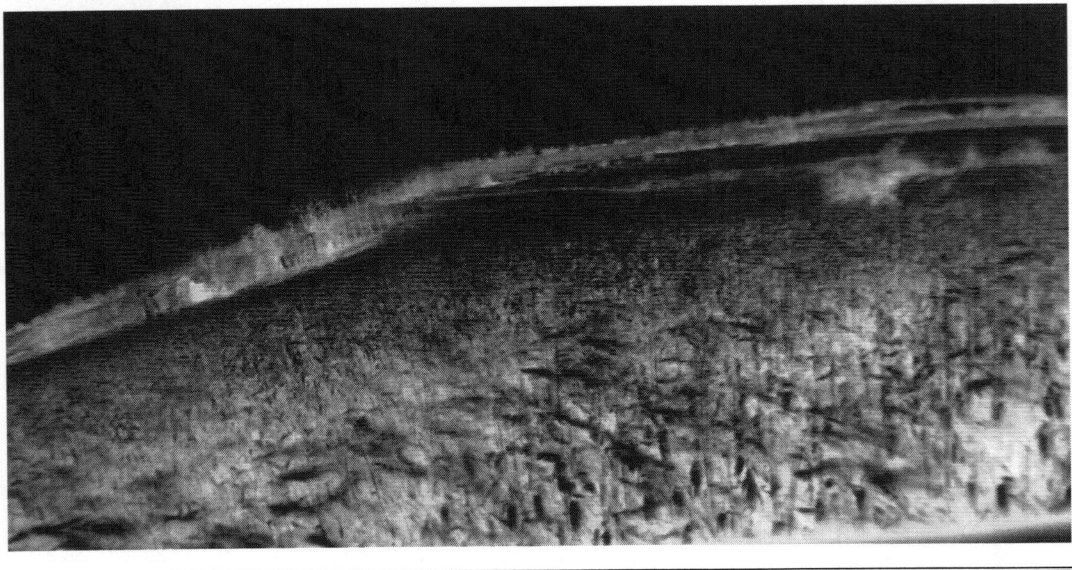

Anamorphic - and unamorphic - camera

Lena Källberg *Frozen dreams © 2008*

The tombola is a combined anamorphic and ordinary cylindrical camera made from a metal can. The pinhole in the lid creates anamorphic pictures and there is a difference in exposure between the top and bottom areas of the image, which can be adjusted by using different kinds of film or paper. Double exposures can be obtained by exposing through both pinholes at the same time.

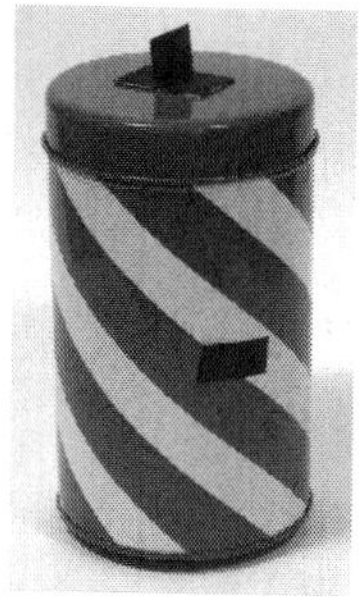

The top pinhole is covered by a magnet instead of black tape, to make it more useful on cold winter days, when electrical tape becomes brittle. After trying out the camera in -18° C, Lena is planning to make an insulating cover for the camera in order to avoid getting frost bitten fingers.

www.pinhole.se

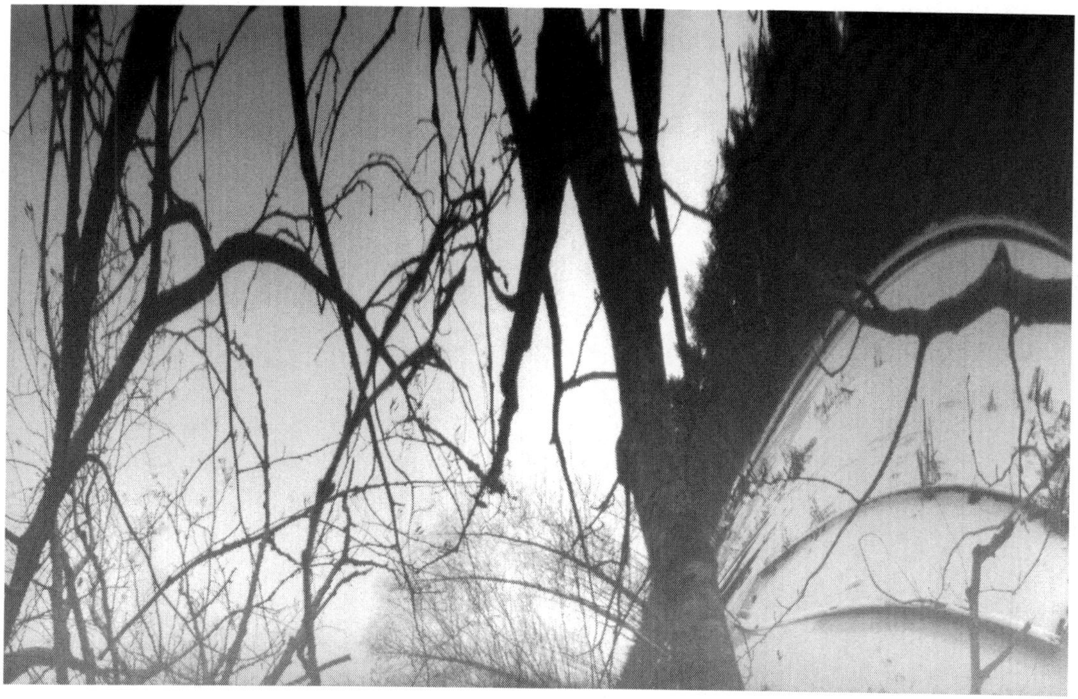

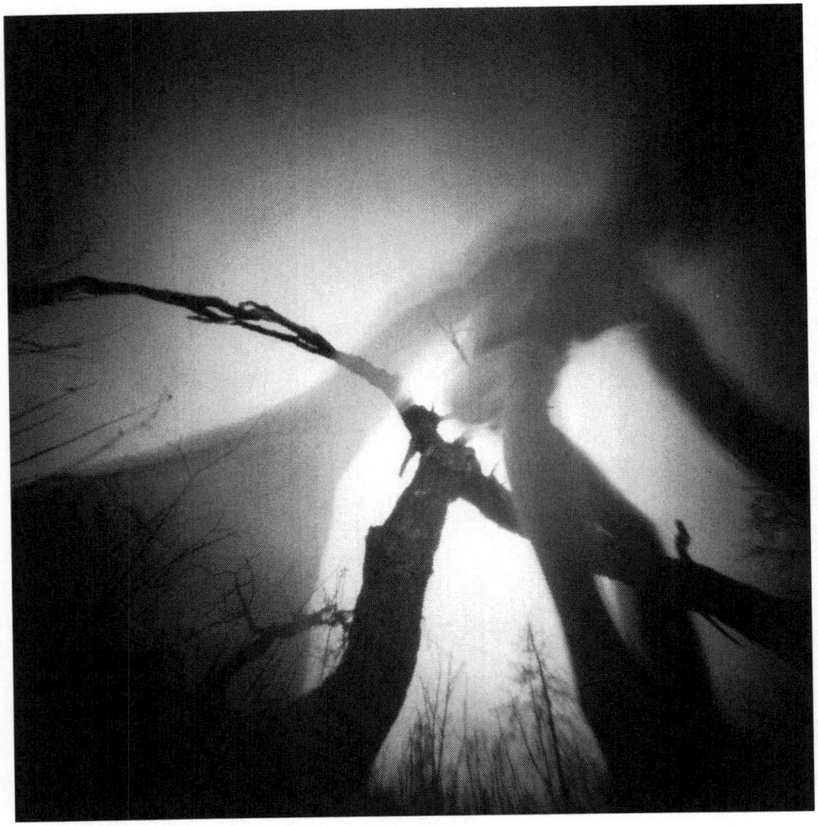

Extreme wide angle

Peter Wiklund

Falling © 2008

One of the advantages of building your own pinhole camera is that you can determine what focal length your camera should have. A short focal length can be especially useful since the pinhole camera has an extreme depth of field, giving sharpness to all parts of the image.

In this image, Peter places his hand only an inch away from the camera and the perspective gets really twisted.

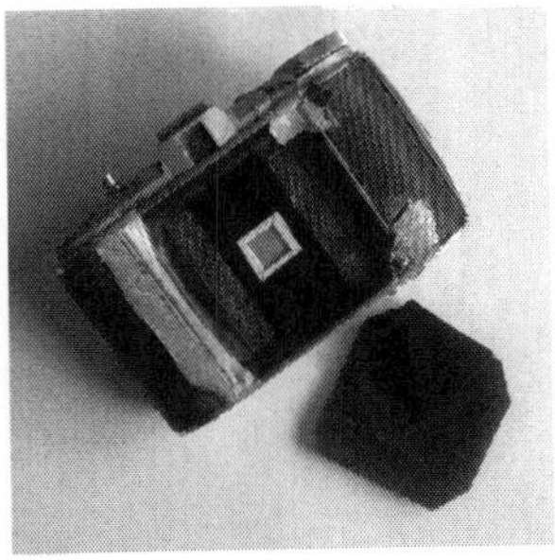

He has built this camera from an old bellows camera, removing the lens and the bellows and replacing them with piece of cardboard with a pinhole plate. The shutter is made of a part of the original camera's carrying case, stuck to the camera front with Velcro ® fastening.

The focal length is approximately 12 mm ($^1/_2$ inch), and since the camera uses ordinary 120-film, the picture area is 56x56 mm (2 $^1/_4$ x 2 $^1/_4$ inches) - making it an extreme wide angle camera.

www.peterpinhole.com

Slit camera

James Guerin *Delphine & Spot © 2008*

James has inserted a slit between the pinhole and the film creating a distorted image. The most common material used to make a slit is Litho film, and to use just a slit, not both a slit and a pinhole like James does.

James uses a technique of winding the film during exposure to create 'photo finish' images.

The camera is a modified 1930s Voightlander folding camera which is easy to find and relatively cheap. The camera's f-stop is f/133, and the effective shutter speed for this shot is 1/30 second. The vertical lines are a result of inconsistent speed of film through the camera.

www.flickr.com/photos/limerick37/

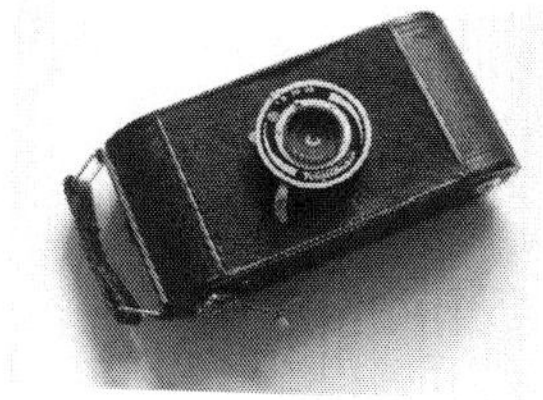

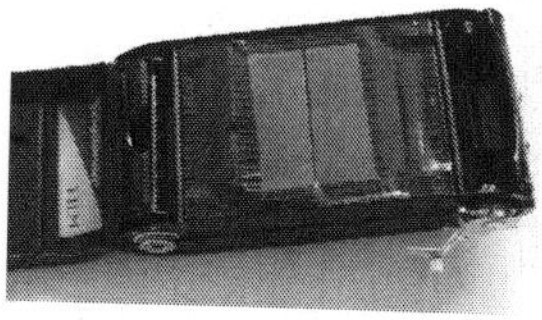

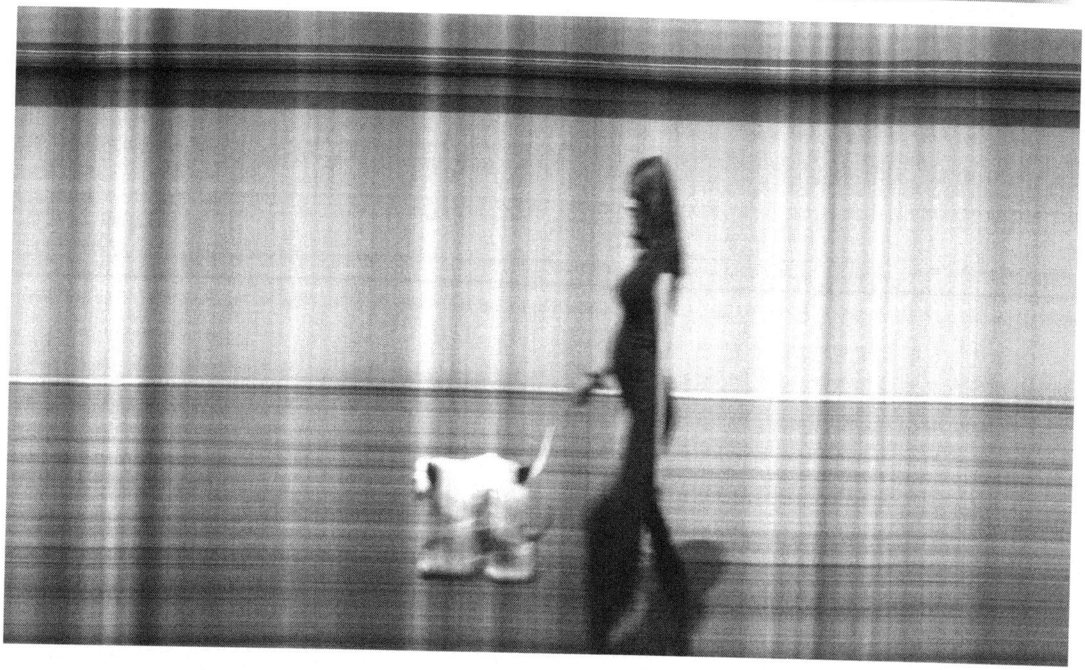

Zone plate camera

William Sadovsky

Winter tree © 2007

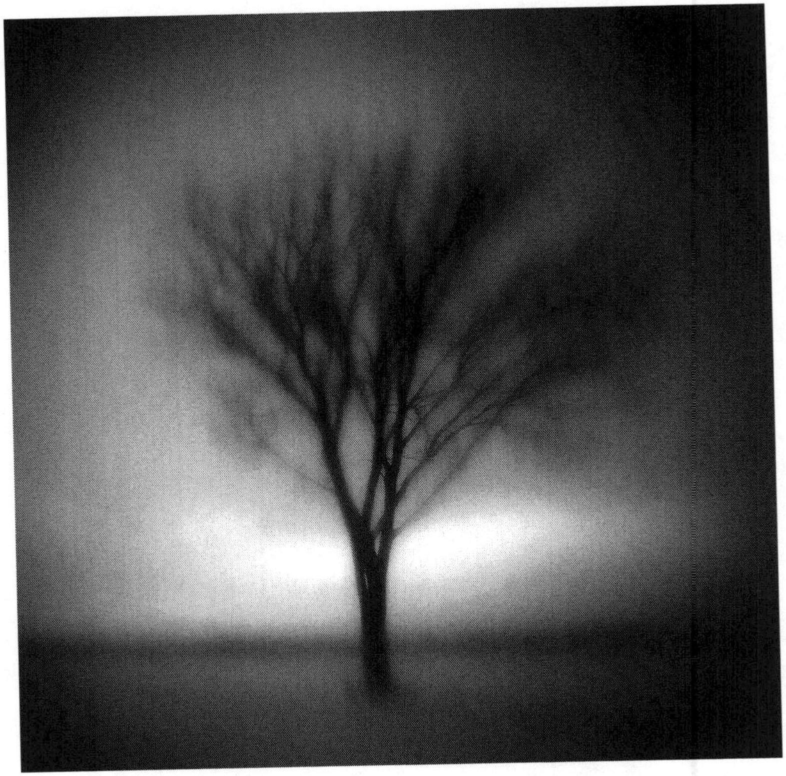

A zone plate is a series of clear and opaque rings which add a soft focus and sometimes a halo to the motif. Zone plates are often made from high contrast film.

William usually uses an old Bronica 2 $^1/_4$ roll film camera with a focal plane shutter and an external focusing tube attached to homemade zone plate lenses. The external focusing tube is what makes this camera special. It allows William to both mount and focus the lens.

William makes the lenses by photographing a zone plate target on high contrast film from varying distances which gives him many focal lengths. The film lenses are then mounted between two pieces of brass plates and then between two pieces of light weight plywood. The lens is attached to the camera with black photo tape.

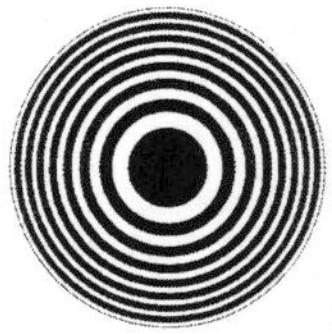

Example of a zone plate

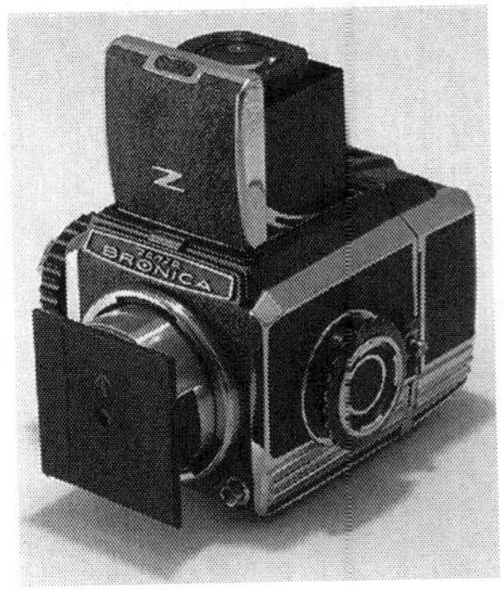

Due to its small size, this camera is much easier to transport and use than his view camera, and the ability to shoot 12 images per roll is also a plus.

www.williamsadovsky.com

Further reading

Here is a short list of books on pinholing:

Pinhole Photography: From Historic Technique to Digital Application
Eric Renner (2008, 4th edition) Focal Press

Adventures with Pinhole and Home-Made Cameras
John Evans (2003) RotoVision

How-To Make Three corrugated 8x10 Pinhole Cameras: Wide-angle, Normal, Telephoto
Anita Chernewski (1999) Pinhole Format Company. Out of print

The Beginner's Guide to Pinhole Photography
Jim Shull (1999) Amherst Media

Primitive Photography: A Guide to Making Cameras, Lenses, and Calotypes
Alan Greene (2001) Focal Press

Internet resources

This list is up to date at the time of printing:

Worldwide Pinhole Photography Day, fun event the last Sunday in April every year - don't miss it!:
www. pinholeday.org

Pinhole Visions, good info site:
www. pinhole.com

F295, exploring photography, articles & forum:
www. f295.org

Mr. Pinhole, brilliant calculators:
www. mrpinhole.com

For more - and definitely up to date - pinhole links, take a look at:
www.AlternativePhotography.com

Further copies

For more copies and bulk discounts go to: AlternativePhotography.com/PinholeToPrint.html

Our other publications

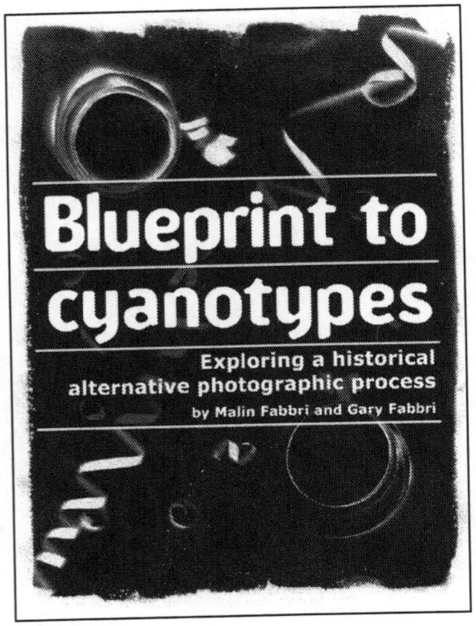

Blueprint to cyanotypes
Exploring a historical alternative photographic process
Written by Malin Fabbri and Gary Fabbri
The cyanotype is often the first alternative process that people try. It is relatively easy and safe enough to nurture a child's interest in photography. It can also be seen as a gateway to further exploration of historic photographic methods. *Blueprint to cyanotypes* is all you will need to get started with cyanotypes. It offers the beginner a step-by-step guide, from choosing material to making the final print. It is full of information and tips. Even the experienced cyanotyper may learn a thing or two.
Format: Paperback, 68 pages, full color, ISBN: 978-1-4116-9838-3
Go to: AlternativePhotography.com/BlueprintToCyanotypes.html

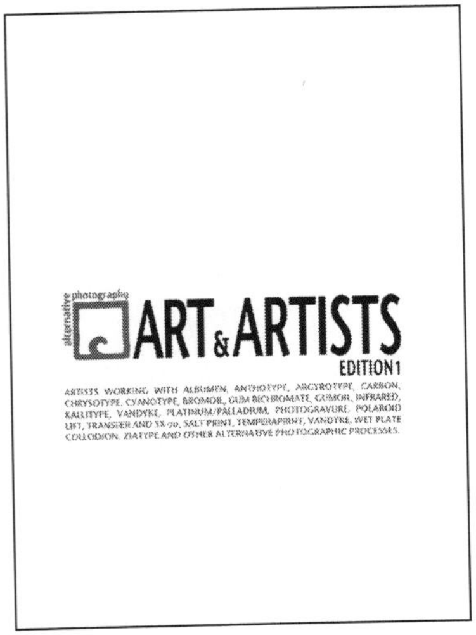

Alternative Photography: Art and Artists, Edition I
Edited by Malin Fabbri
Alternative Photography: Art and Artists, Edition I highlights the work of over 100 of today's most active photographers working with alternative processes. Discover how the different processes create a unique look in a print, and get an insight into how the processes function. Artists introduce themselves, their work and why they chose the qualities of that particular process. A wide variety of processes, concepts and ideas can be found. And, the purpose of this book? To inspire.
Format: Paperback and hardback, 238 pages, full color
Go to: AlternativePhotography.com/ArtAndArtists.html

15460361R00026

Printed in Great Britain
by Amazon